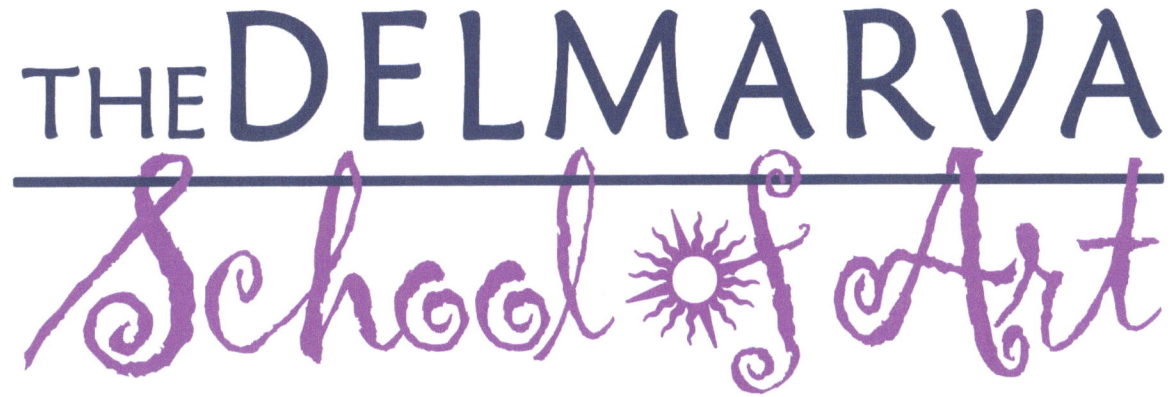

THE DELMARVA School of Art

By Dana Kester-McCabe

All artwork presented in this publication belongs to the artists who created them.

Book Design by Dana Kester-McCabe and Stephanie Fowler.

This book was set in 12 point Columbia Medium, with titles in Gigi,
and subtitles in Maiandra.

ISBN 978-1-62806-146-8   (print | paperback)

Library of Congress Control Number 2017962611

Dedication

To the artists of Delmarva who have inspired me
with their skills, creativity, and humility...

Thank you also to Lisa Challenger and the members of the
Tourism, Arts, Downtown Development collective
and eatdrinkbuyart.com for their support.

Contents & Artist Images

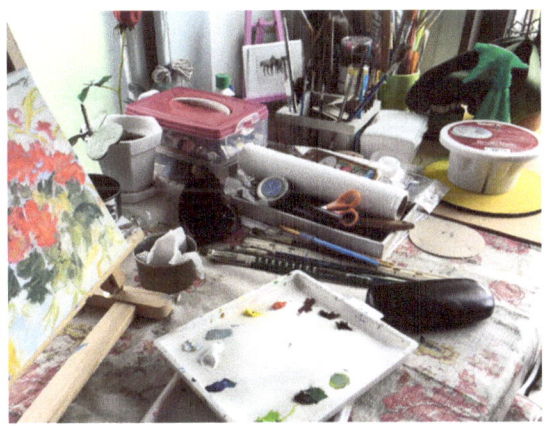

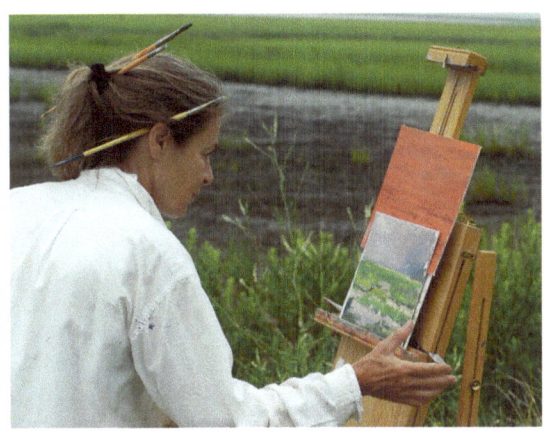

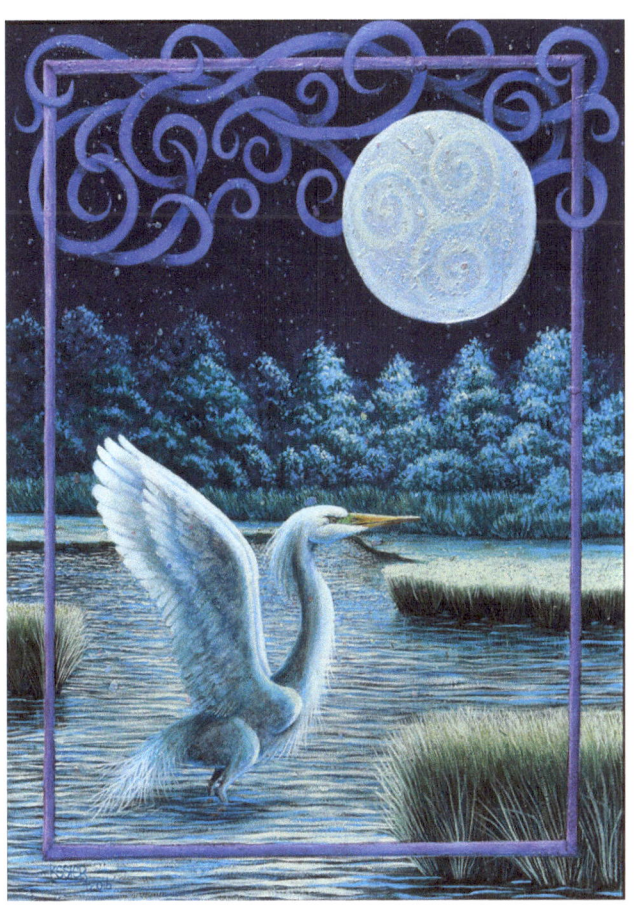

Introduction

In 2009, I began writing and producing the Delmarva Almanac, an online magazine covering the rich culture and natural beauty of the region where I live on the Eastern Shore of Maryland. Within a year I was producing short video interviews with local artists. Since then I have been lucky enough to have in depth conversations about creativity and the artist's life with 112 talented people all here on the Delmarva Peninsula. Some of these people worked in the visual arts while others were in theater and music. Though I have mostly made a living producing graphics, websites, and commercial writing, my own background and my bachelor's degree is in painting. So, these talks were fascinating for me as well as my audience. In some ways, it was like getting a master's degree in fine art.

Eventually I found funding to produce the Delmarva Almanac as a half hour weekly radio show on the local NPR station - Delmarva Public Radio - out of Salisbury, Maryland. This was a great experience, but when funding challenges arose I took stock and decided that it was time to go back to my earliest passion. I had come away from all of those artist interviews really missing time for my own painting. So, I am returning to that work. In the meantime, I also realized that I had learned many valuable lessons from these talented people which would make a great book for art lovers and artists alike. This is it: The Delmarva School of Art.

Forty-six of the visual artists I interviewed are represented in this book. They are a good cross section of the various forms and genres being practiced here today. Through samples of their work, excerpts from our conversations, and my observations, I will share with you what I learned in the last seven years.

My approach to the interviews was to ask questions that simply made it easy for these artists to tell their stories, and then I just sat back to listen. In order to produce a five-to-eight-minute-long video, I usually spent about an hour talking

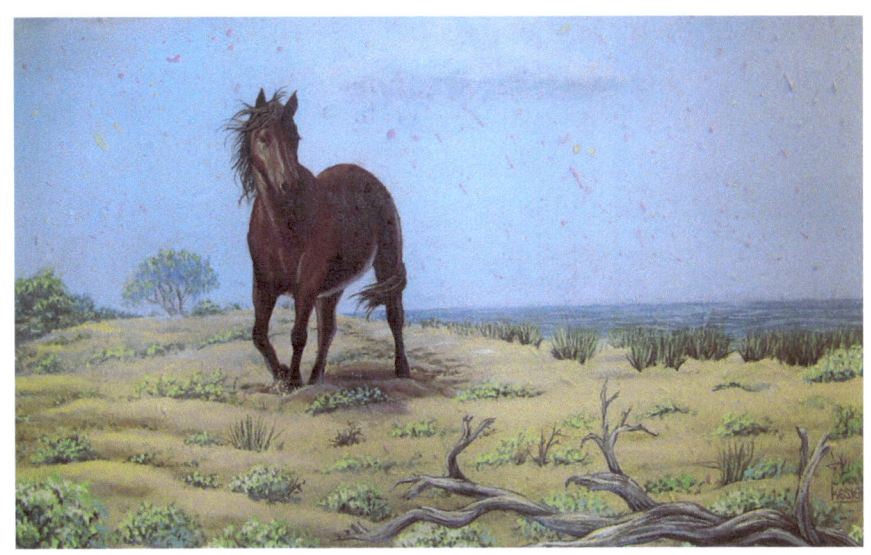

Dana Kester-McCabe
Charcoal Pony
(2013) Acrylics

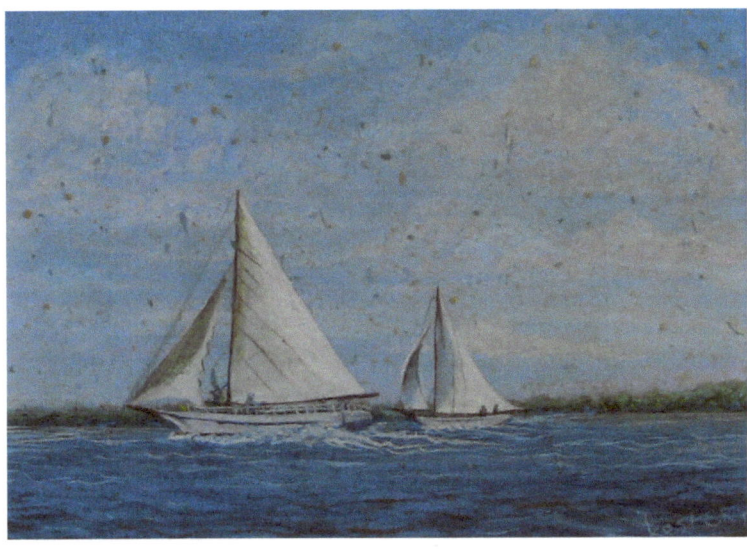

Dana Kester-McCabe
Skipjacks
(2012) Acrylics

to each of them. Sometimes our discussions went much longer because we were having so much fun talking about creative subjects which were dear to our hearts.

The first chapter of this book is focused on those artists whose work is all about storytelling: the experiences they want to share, or the heritage of the place where they live. The second chapter showcases the lessons provided by those artists who are not afraid to color outside the lines. It takes courage to share one's innermost ideas and emotions. To make a living doing that requires a certain amount of fearlessness.

Most of the artists I met are much more process oriented than they are product oriented. They love the act of making art. However, that does not mean they are not committed to the quality of what they produce. Quite the opposite. Creative work requires a sense of discipline and dedication. Surprisingly it is that discipline that provides the greatest freedom of expression. That relationship between personal discipline and a liberated creativity is the subject of the next chapter.

The light and coastal lifestyle here have inspired many people to move to the Delmarva region just to make art. The next chapter of this book is about those artists whose subject matter is directly tied to the beauty of their home and what many have called *the land of pleasant living*. Finally, in the last chapter, I will share some lessons I learned about what it means to be an artist and creative living.

Before we proceed to what we can learn from these artists, let's begin with a brief look back at the history of art here on Delmarva. This will set the stage for the environment that has become the current Delmarva art scene. There is precious little surviving evidence of the arts and crafts of Delmarva's earliest inhabitants. The Nanticoke Indian Museum in Millsboro, Delaware, has perhaps the most comprehensive collection of our region's native arrow heads or stone axe blades, and pottery dating back to 8,000 B.C. The Nabb Center at Salisbury University and

The Chesapeake Maritime Museum in St. Michael's also have artifact collections. Sadly, much of the culture of our many local tribes is otherwise now lost.

The most visible tribute to our native people are two "Whispering Giants", large carved wood totem style sculptures, one in Bethany Beach, Delaware, and the other in Ocean City, Maryland. The visionary artist who created these statues in the 1970's, Peter Wolf Toth, was not a Native American. He and his family escaped the Soviet takeover of Hungary in 1956 when he was a just a small child. He grew up as a refugee in Ohio to become an itinerant artist traveling from state to state carving and donating his Indian sculptures to local communities. Peter sees this work as a calling to honor displaced indigenous people everywhere and to thank the country that gave his family a permanent refuge from war and poverty.

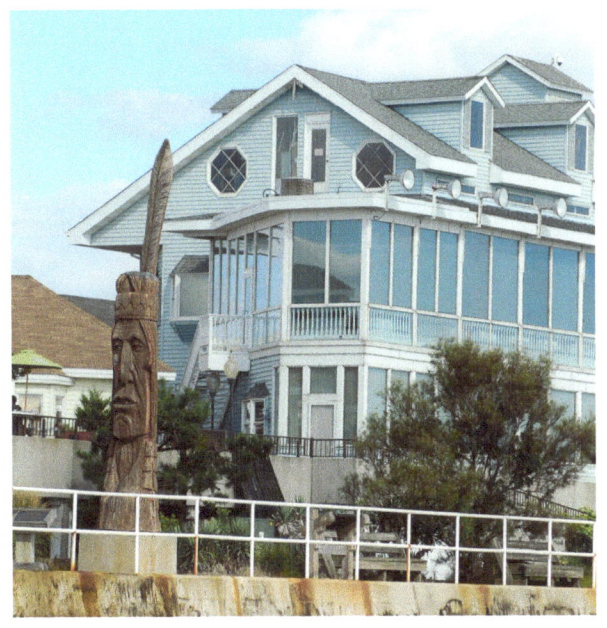

Peter Toth - Nanticoke
(1976) Carved Oak

There also is not much artwork to be found from the colonial period of Delmarva. A few homes that have been preserved as historical sites may have some embroidery samplers and painted furniture, but European settlers in this region lived a pretty frugal lifestyle that did not afford a great deal of artwork. Only the wealthiest families could afford painted portraits and objects d'art imported from abroad. Visual artists may have been scarce, but the first known record of a play being performed in the colonies was actually here in Pungoteague, Virginia in 1665. We know about it because there are written records of the players being acquitted in court on charges of illicit behavior for performing their play which was called "The Bear and The Cub".

The earliest artist of note to hail from this region was famed portrait artist Charles Wilson Peale. He was born in 1741 in the town of Chester, in Queen Anne's County Maryland. His mother moved their family when he was very young, to the Annapolis area after they were abandoned by his father.

The Biggs Museum, in Dover Delaware has perhaps the definitive collection of fine arts and crafts created in this region from the colonial period up through the end of the 19th century. It was opened by collector Sewell C. Biggs in 1993. The region enjoyed some success with basketry, button making, and holiday wreaths during the late 1800's and early 1900's. Though there must certainly have been people producing various other forms of arts and crafts here, their work has mostly otherwise not survived except perhaps in a few private family collections.

During the early 20th Century artists arrived from eastern Pennsylvania and Wilmington, Delaware, to take advantage of the coastal beauty and rural privacy of Rehoboth Beach. That is when Delmarva's art scene really got started. For years illustrator Howard Pyle, of Brandywine School fame, had a retreat there, where his students visited, including N.C. Wyeth. One of those pupils, Ethel Pennewill Brown, had her own cottage in the same vacation community. Ethel was a Wilmington native who was a successful women's magazine illustrator. In 1928, she got together with other artists living or working nearby and began holding exhibitions at what was then known as the Village Improvement Association on the boardwalk in Rehoboth Beach.

Ethel believed that her summer home was the perfect spot to form an artist colony. Not only was it a lovely place to work, but it attracted its own clientele:

tourists wanting souvenirs to remember their stay at the beach. Artists Eugenia Eckford Rhoads, Betty Harrington Macdonald, Jack Lewis, and Howard Schroeder all agreed. Louise Corkran and her husband Colonel Wilbur Corkran, an architect and real estate developer, were also pivotal members of this group. They purchased a 200-acre property which had been a working plantation as early as 1675 and restored its historic 1743 cypress-shingled homestead. Some say a man named Peter Marsh had built it as a base of operations to search unsuccessfully for the treasure of pirate Captain William Kidd who had operated in the area. An old farm house was moved there from another location, and this became the complex's working studio. The entire property eventually became the Rehoboth Art League.

At its grand opening in 1938, Annie Pile (the widow of Howard) signed her name to the studio door. Others in attendance followed her lead, with some adding small pictorial flourishes. Ethel added a lotus blossom. A well-known cartoonist of the day, Earl Chesney, drew a captain's hat and pipe. Since that time almost three hundred artists, and guests have signed those doors, which have been preserved and put on display. Through the next decades the Rehoboth Art League has had a number of renovations; many, many art exhibits; and a growing permanent collection of visual art including work by Howard Pyle, Howard Schroeder, and Ethel Penniwell Brown among others. The League's annual member show attracts artists and collectors from around the world.

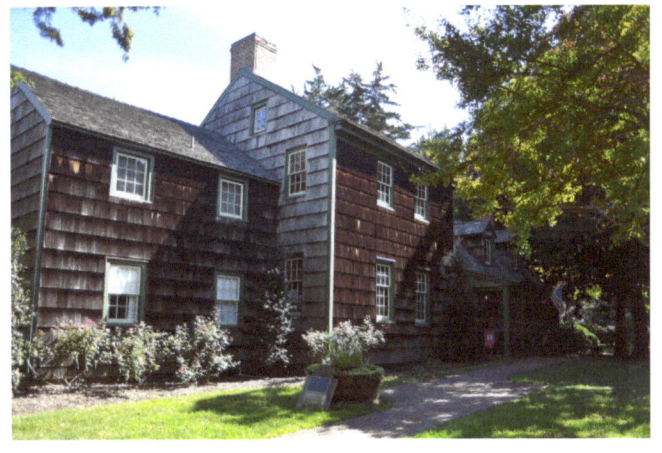

Dana Kester-McCabe
Rehoboth Art League
(2017) Digital Photograph

Elsewhere on Delmarva, during the same time the artists' colony was taking off in Rehoboth Beach, one particular folk art was blossoming along the shores of the Chesapeake Bay. Wildfowl hunting was a very popular pastime and tourist attraction for the region. Carved wooden decoys became a cottage industry. Most of the wooden ducks and geese were rudimentary and not terribly detailed. They fulfilled their purpose of attracting birds to ponds and marsh lagoons where they were set afloat. But, the more realistic they were the better they worked. Carvers began to compete to see who could make the most lifelike decoys. Hunters began to collect them not just for their use in the field, but for their great beauty.

In Crisfield, Maryland, Lem and Steve Ward, like their father before them, made their living as barbers. Though they had their own shop, they still lived close to the land, hunting and fishing. They began carving decoys for their own use, but their skills began to get a reputation and so they developed a side business selling their decoys. Their craft helped sustain them through the Great Depression and led them to acclaim as folk artists through nationwide carving contests. Despite that success they did not give up their day job. They retired as barbers in 1965 when they were in their 70's. Not surprisingly they also sang in a barbershop quartet and even took part in musical competitions.

Though the sign on their decoy shop said: L.T. Ward & Brothers - Wildfowl Counterfeiters in Wood, they were indeed genuine artists

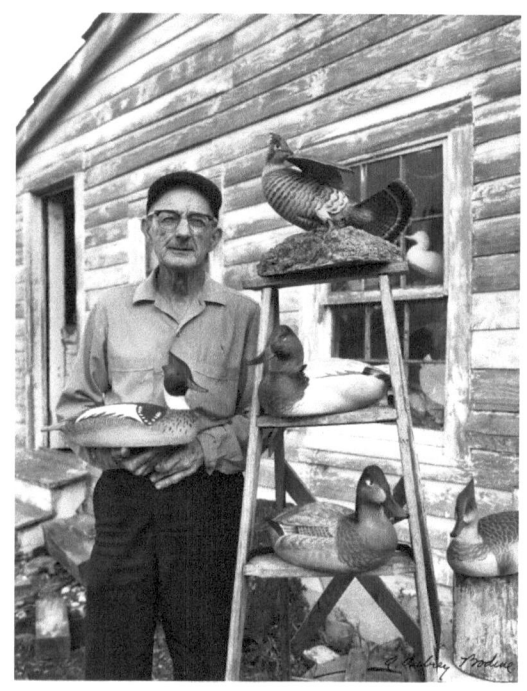

Aubrey A. Bodine - Lem Ward
(1965) Silver Gelatin Photograph
© Jennifer B. Bodine
Courtesy of aaubreybodine.com

inside and out. Their workshop in Crisfield is now an historical site. And, the Ward Museum was begun at Salisbury University in 1968 to preserve their decoys and their story. It has grown into one of the country's preeminent museums for wildfowl art. They hold an annual worldwide competition every April in nearby Ocean City showcasing working decoys and decorative sculptures.

On the other side of the peninsula is an equally well-regarded competition at the annual Waterfowl Festival in Easton, Maryland which is held every Fall. Also in Easton, is the Academy of Fine Arts which opened its doors in 1958. They are known for their classes and for supporting both the visual and performing arts. The Academy also holds prestigious art competitions and can boast a permanent collection including prints by Impressionist Pierre Bonnard, and pop art expressionist Robert Rauschenberg.

When I first moved to Delmarva in 1980, the most predominant art form seemed to be those famed duck decoys along with paintings of nautical or coastal scenes, seashells, and the wild horses of Assateague. These were popular with tourists, so they seemed to be the subjects that most galleries here would take a chance on. Many local artists entered paintings in the annual federal duck stamp competition at the time. Full sized prints of the winning

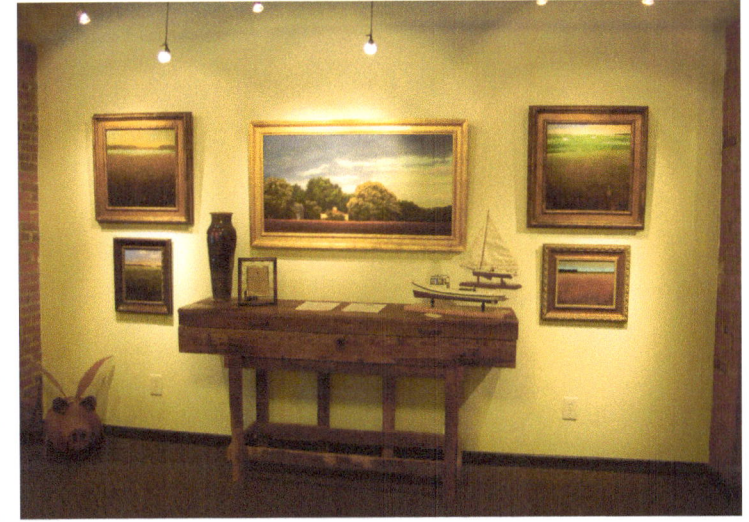

Dana Kester-McCabe
Bishop's Stock Gallery - Snow Hill
(2015) Digital Photograph

original paintings for the stamps had become very fashionable. Since the 1970's the Ward Museum, the Biggs Museum, The Academy, and the Rehoboth Art League have been the torch bearers for the visual arts here. But, a growing number of galleries and community art leagues have been working valiantly too.

Indeed, the visual arts are alive and well here. There are world class galleries like Bishop Stock in Snow Hill, the South Street Gallery in Easton, the Carla Massoni Gallery in Chestertown, and the Ocean City Center for The Arts. The family run Turner Foundry and Gallery in Melfa, Virginia, is famous for its grand bronze wildlife sculptures which can be seen in public gardens all around the region and well beyond. Berlin, Denton, and St. Michael's in Maryland; Onancock, and Cape Charles, Virginia; along with Dover, Milton, and Milford in Delaware all have flourishing artist communities. These and other towns here have created arts districts to encourage artists and related businesses. They host monthly art strolls where galleries and restaurants have special events.

Most of the counties here have thriving art leagues where hobbyists and emerging professionals can take classes to hone their crafts like the Worcester County Arts Council in Berlin and the Fiber Arts Center in Denton Maryland, the Eastern Shore's Own Art Center in Bell Haven Virginia, and the Mispillion Art League in Milford, Delaware. Sculptors, ceramicists, and glass artists are becoming more and more common. We have fine art

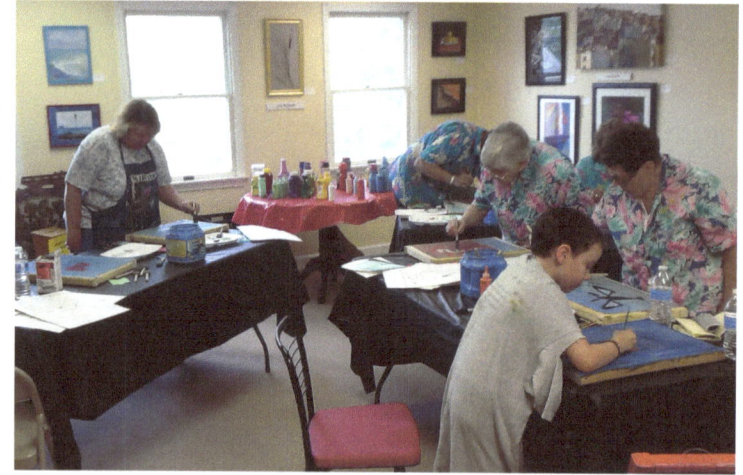

John Iampieri
St. Michael's Workshop
(2016) Digital Photograph

jewelers and fiber artists. There are painters working in every genre from realism to pop-art to abstract expressionism, and everything in between or beyond.

By far the most popular form of painting is Impressionism. Delmarva Impressionists have the ocean, marshes, and quaint towns to provide endless inspiration. As you read further, many of the artists you will meet have settled here just to take advantage of the abundant light reflected on the waters that surround us. Many are plein air painters who work outdoors the way the French Impressionists did. There are annual plein air competitions in several towns on Delmarva where spectators can watch the artists at work and purchase their finished pieces at "wet paint" sales.

Yes, a great deal has changed here since I arrived in 1980 and even in the last seven years since I began interviewing local artists. Those artists themselves are the best evidence I can give you that the arts have blossomed and we are so much the better for it. I am sure that I personally will grow and benefit from what they taught me for a long time.

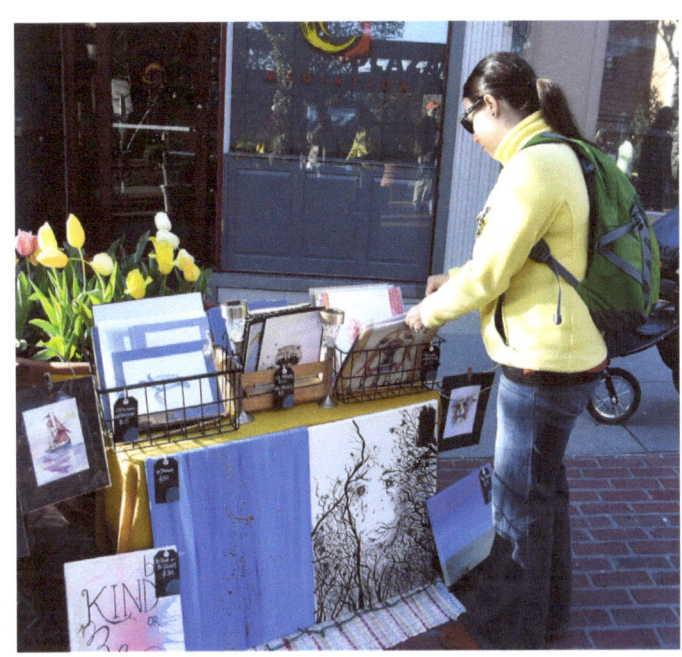

The best way I can recommend how to learn from these talented individuals is to simply enjoy looking at their work. So that is the focus of this book. Let the work speak for itself.

Dana Kester-McCabe
Salisbury Third Friday Art Stroll
(2016) Digital Photograph

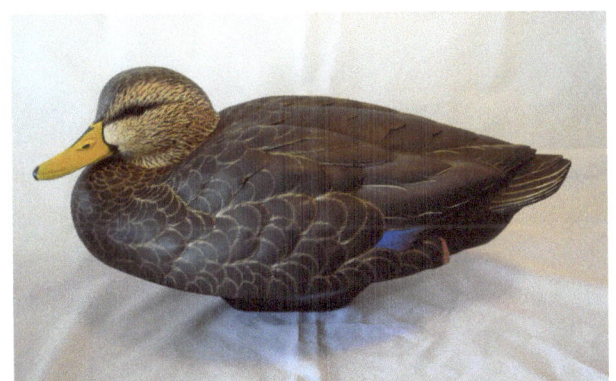

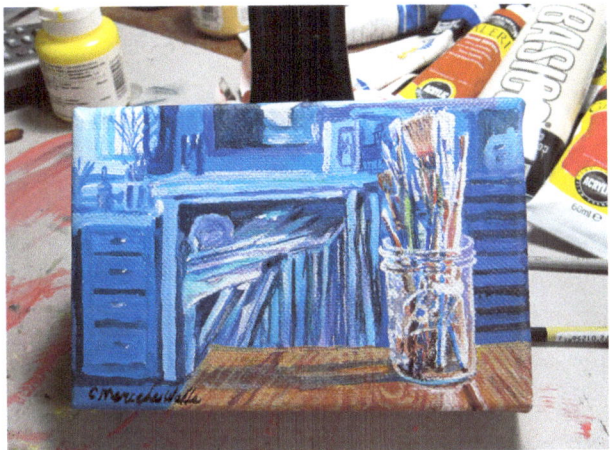

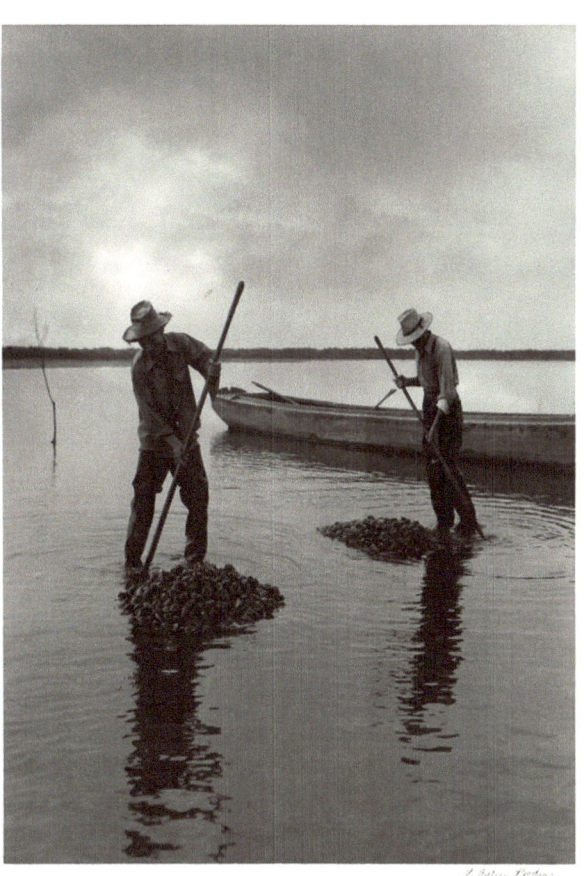

Telling Our Stories

The heart of most art forms is to communicate. Many of Delmarva's storyteller artists are conveying a common sense of loss and longing for a simpler time. Others are simply lifting up moments in time they want to preserve forever. Like artists everywhere they use their unique perceptions to tell those stories only they can tell through hand crafted mediums.

One artist who loved to tell visual stories about the waters and people of Delmarva, was the late *Baltimore Sun* photographer A. Aubrey Bodine. He never lived here but he spent a great deal of time here. His daughter Jennifer does live here in Denton where she continues to sell prints and books by her father. She told me: "Just looking at his photography, so much of it is from the Eastern Shore. He was a big fan of the watermen, in particular, and enjoyed going out on boats with them and talking to them and learning about the community. He was fearless for a man who could not swim. He could have gone over the side any number of times. In fact, his most famous "Choptank Oyster Dredgers" was taken during a Nor'easter. He was out on a skipjack with a large format five by seven camera, balancing himself while everything was whipping around, taking the picture, which turned out to be a world-famous picture."

To tell a good story the way Aubrey did, an artist needs to first be curious about their subject. Artists often ask themselves if an idea is worth spending time on: Why should anyone want to see a picture of this? Why would someone care about this enough to stop and look at it, let alone consider buying it? Plein air painter Debra Howard told me: "I feel very strongly: only paint things you are interested in because if you're not interested in it nobody's going to be interested in it." She takes just three colors red, yellow, and blue, to mix a myriad of hues that evoke the magical light she sees along our countryside.

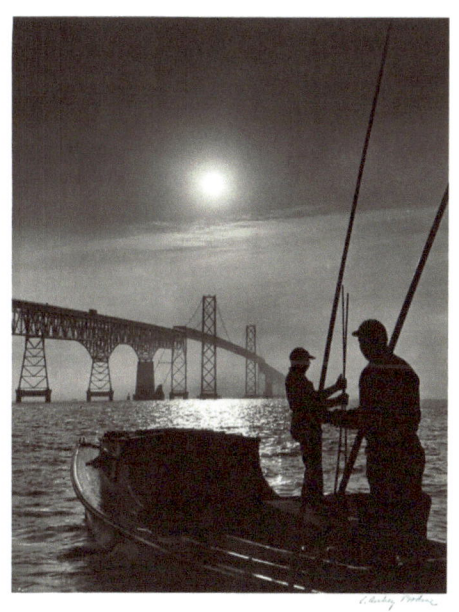

Oyster Tongers
(1965) Silver Gelatin Photograph

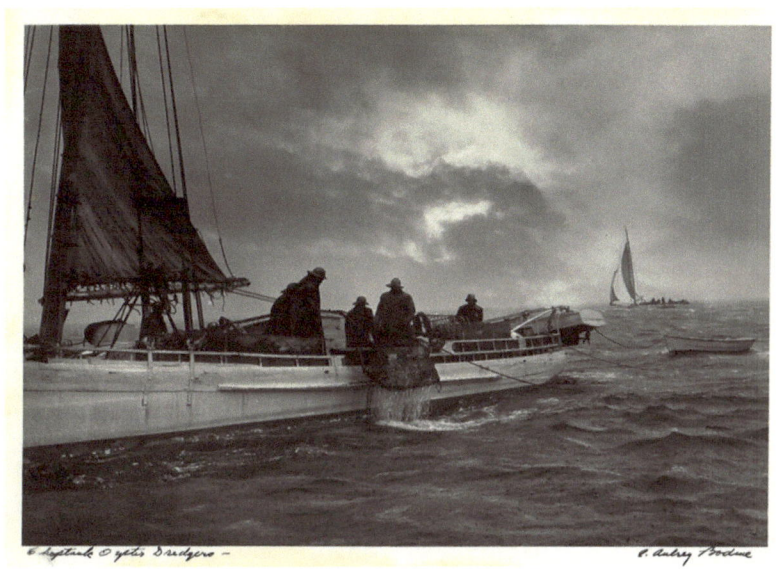

Choptank Oyster Dredgers
(1948) Silver Gelatin Photograph

Debra Howard

artistdebrahoward.com

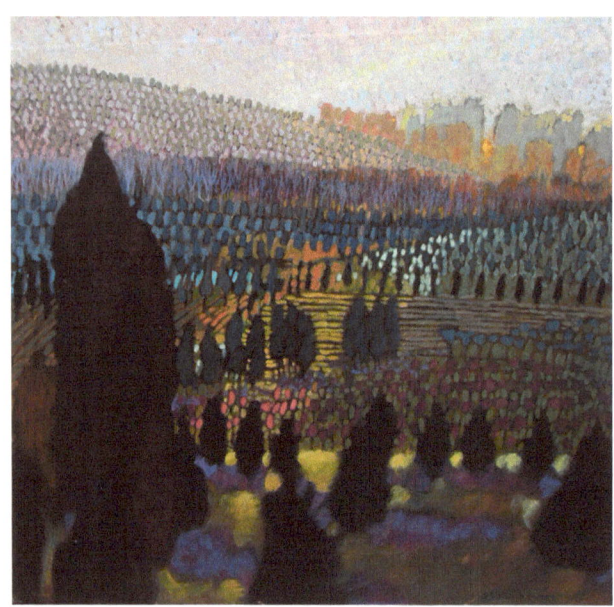

The Tree Farm
(2015) Oil

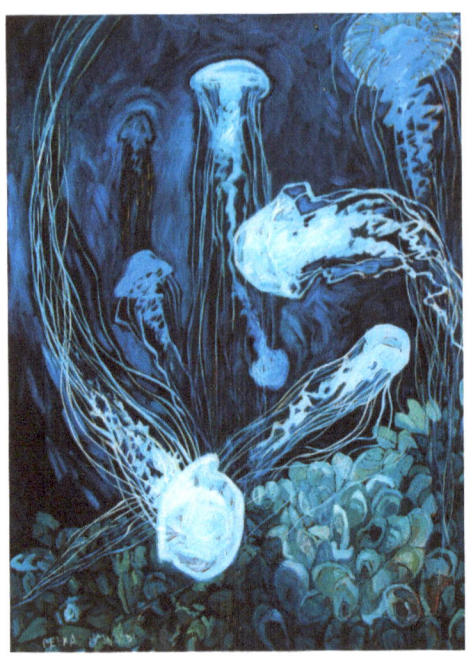

Sea Nettles Over An Oysterbed
(2016) Oil

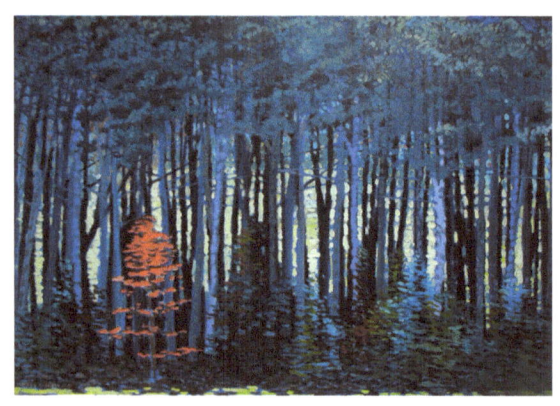

Maple At The Edge Of The Wood
(2015) Oil

Sometimes it is hard for an artist to choose a subject because they get ideas wherever they go. Geraldine McKeown, of Elkton Maryland, mostly paints landscapes but finds inspiration everywhere, whether it is in a stack of bushel baskets, or on a rainy country road. She said her "mind is just always looking at the world as subject matter for a painting."

C. Mercedes Walls (Cathy) paints scenes she encounters in her daily life in and around Milford, Delaware: people in a café, a couple walking through town, or musicians in a pub. She wants to show "life in this location". She has discovered that some of the most enduring imagery is not of monumental historical events, or of quaintly perfect or beautiful scenes, but of the everyday experiences we can all relate to.

Often storytelling is about recording something so that it will not be lost. Salisbury painter Keith Whitelock, captures imagery long associated with a life on Delmarva which seems to be fading away. A master watercolorist, his subjects include the boats, marshes, and hunting scenes which represent the life of Delmarva's watermen. He loves the texture of an abandoned boat lying on a marsh with its still bright white paint flaking off to reveal a weathered hull the color of grey driftwood. "There's something about these old boats and shanties that are not all prettied-up. I never realized early on, how quickly these boats and things would go away. All of my subject matter is disappearing. It's going away in leaps and bounds."

Rich Smoker, from Marion Station, works in a genre that also is at risk of fading away. He creates wooden decoys and bird sculptures. The genre is still popular but not like it was a few decades ago. Rich describes his job as trying to "bring life out of a dead block of wood". He says as a youngster he learned that "a man who works with his hands is a laborer. A man who works with his hands and his mind is a craftsman. And a man who works with his hands, his mind, and his heart is an

Geraldine McKeown

mckeownart.com

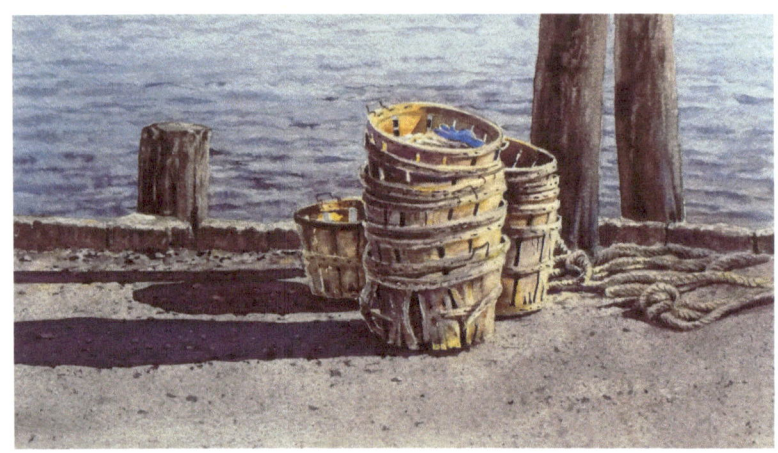

Bay Baskets
(2017) Watercolor

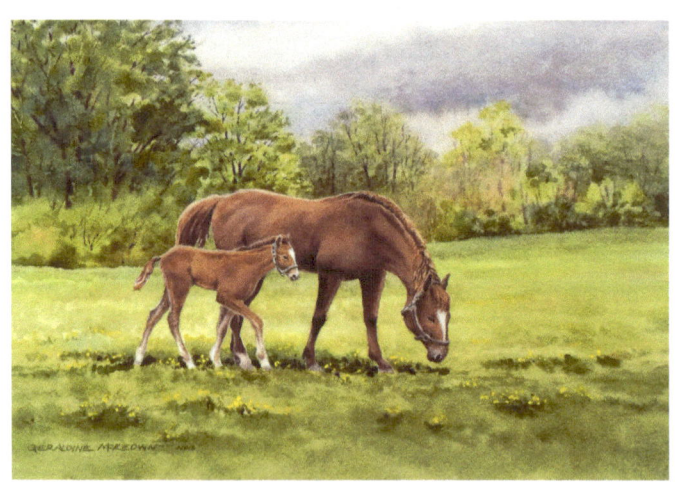

Rainy Monday
(2017) Watercolor

Spring Foal
(2017) Watercolor

18

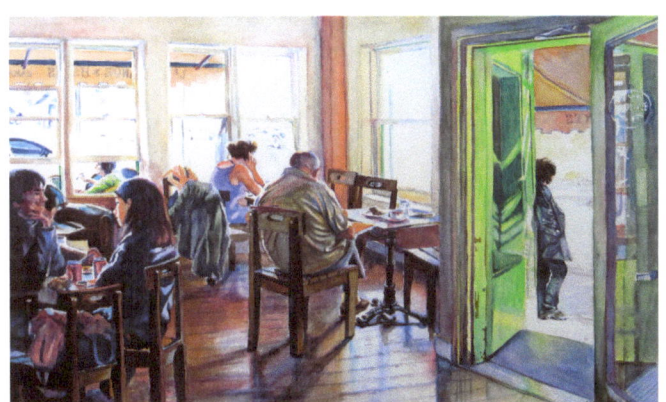

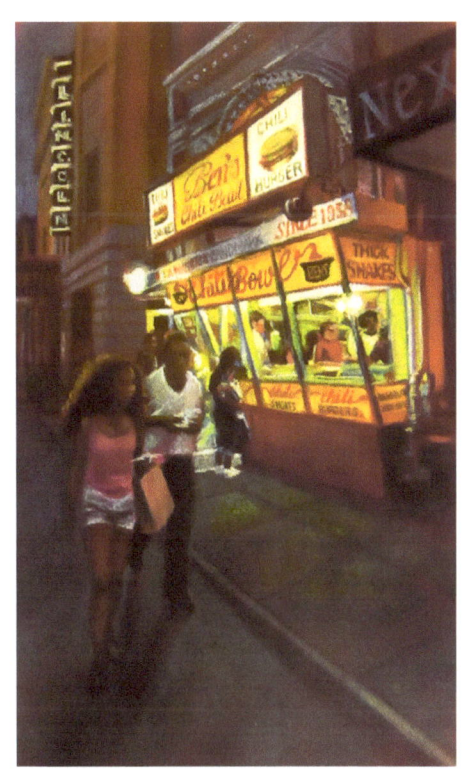

Journey To Soul
(2015) Oil

Ben's Chili Bowl
(2014) Pastel

Alone Together
(2013) Watercolor

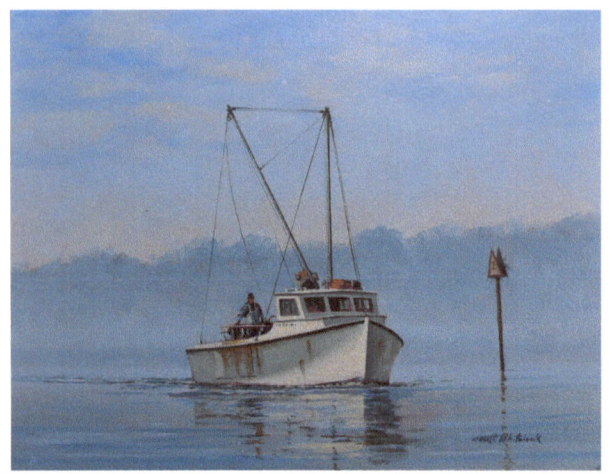

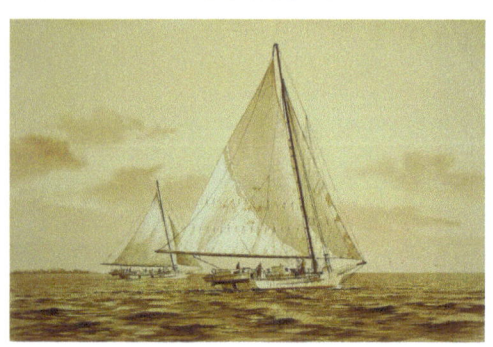

Returning Waterman
(2017) Oil

Sepia Skipjack
(2015) Watercolor

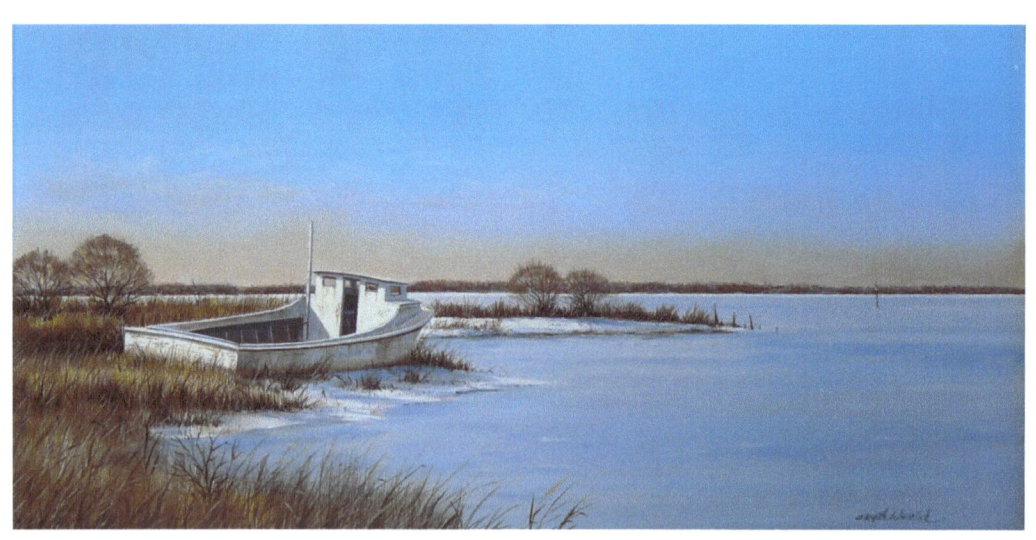

Frozen Creek
(2016) Acrylic

Rich Smoker

facebook.com/
rwsmoker.wildfowl.carving

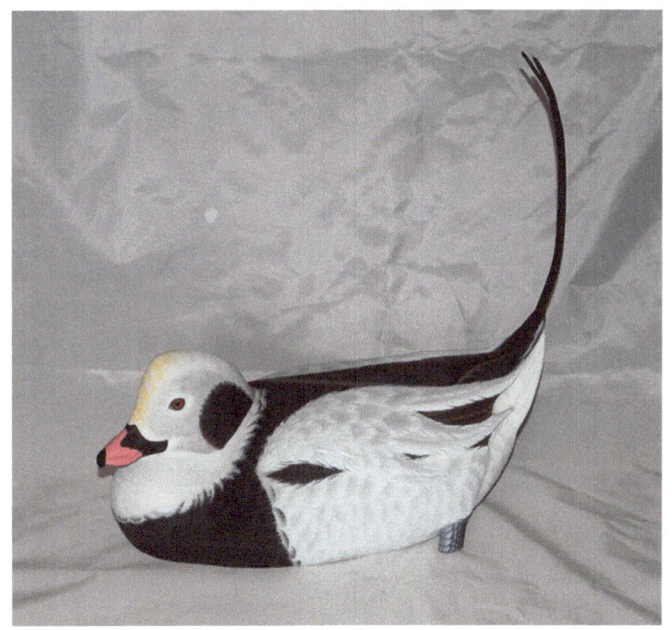

Old Squaw (also known as Long Tailed Duck)
(2010) Acrylic and gouache on carved Tupelo

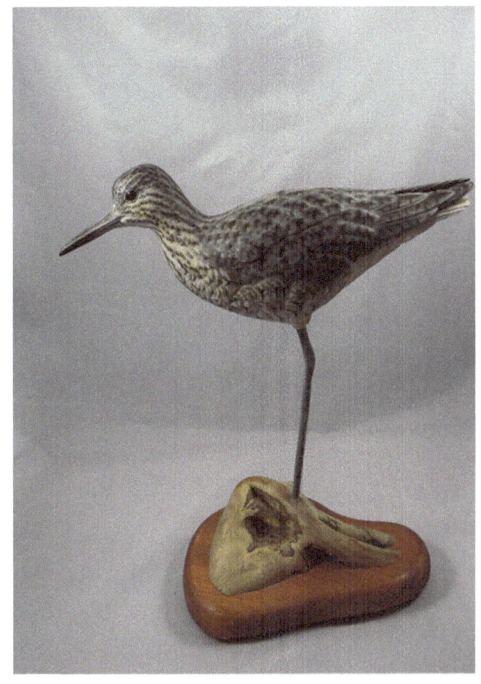

Willet
(2010) Acrylic and gouache on
carved Tupelo

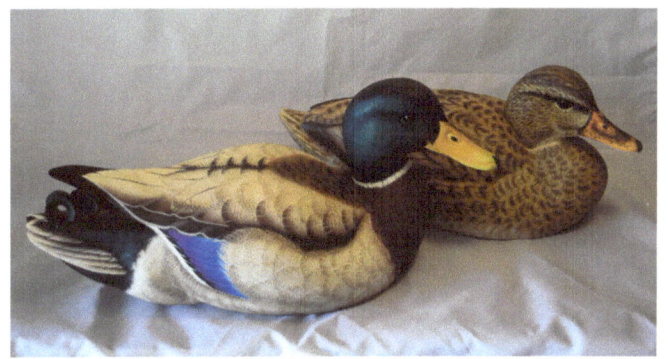

Mallard Pair
(2010) Acrylic paint on carved Tupelo

artist." Rich does not limit his carvings to just ducks and geese. He says his favorite bird to carve is always "the next one". Once the carving is finished he enjoys getting lost in the process of painting them. The story he is telling is about a love for the mysterious beauty of the wildlife all around us which we do not always take time to appreciate and whose future has no guarantee.

A few years ago, Keith and Rich might have been considered quintessential Eastern Shore artists. Today their traditional subject matter is still greatly appreciated but like cream rising to the top of a bottle of milk, so have other genres of art here risen to join theirs. Using a more contemporary style and color palette, Stevensville painter Maureen Bannon tells a similar story. She chooses quiet pastoral scenes that seem to have a story to tell: a boat yard, marsh grass poking through a fence, or a garden fountain and flowers in sunlight.

Photography by Allen Sklar, of Bishopville Maryland, allows the viewer to see wildlife that they might not otherwise ever see in person. He tells the story behind his photograph which recorded the unusual visit of a Snowy Owl to our area. "Snowy Owls are not only rare but seldom seen. This bird was originally tagged in Delaware, but eventually was injured at a Maryland Airport. Transferred to two rehab facilities over six months, it's wing was surgically repaired and it was released on Assateague. The expression of its first taste of freedom is priceless!" The majesty of Allen's picture of the bird in flight not only tells us something amazing about nature. It also connects us to a liberated feeling we all wish we could experience.

Accurately depicting what an artist has seen or experienced is just one kind of tale to tell. Ric Conn, of Queen Anne's County, is known for his realistic pastel paintings of birds but he has devoted most of his time recently to more expressionistic images depicting contemporary young women. It is hard to interpret the story Ric is trying to tell. Ric says he hopes that viewers either love or hate his work. Either extreme helps him achieve his goal of simply moving the audience.

Maureen Bannon

bannonfineart.com

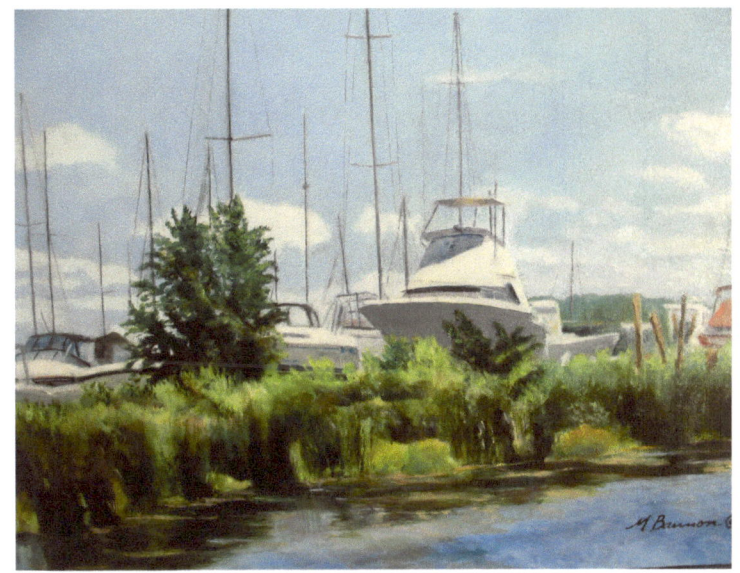

Lippencott Marina
(2015) Oils

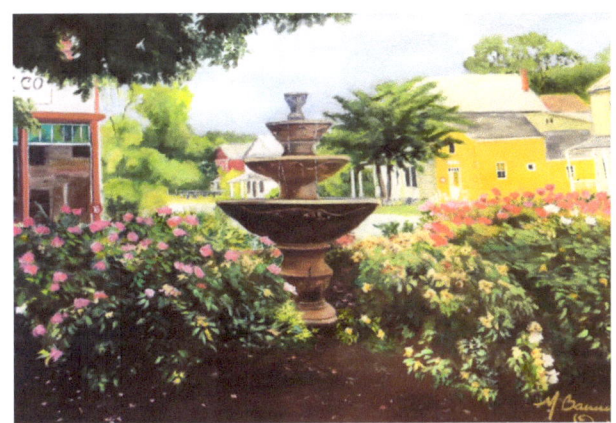

Sense of Home
(2017) Oils

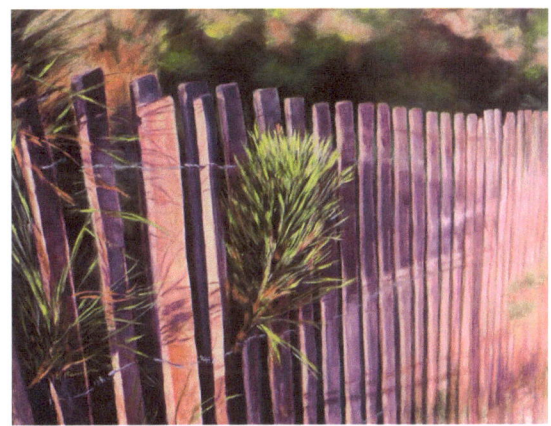

Beach Fence
(2011) Oils

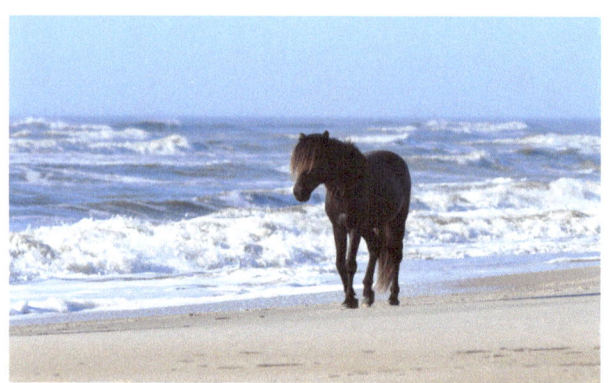

Black Stallion
(2015) Digital Photograph

Allen Sklar

assateaguephotos.com

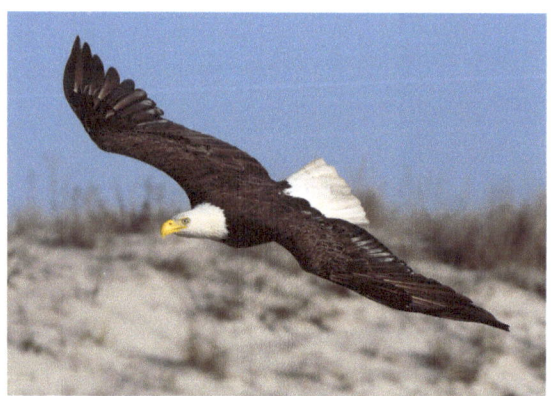

Eagle
(2017) Digital Photograph

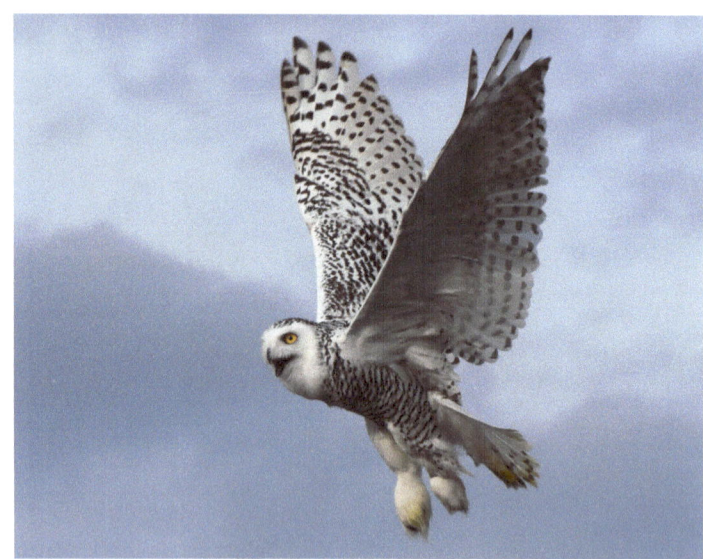

Snowy Owl
(2016) Digital Photograph

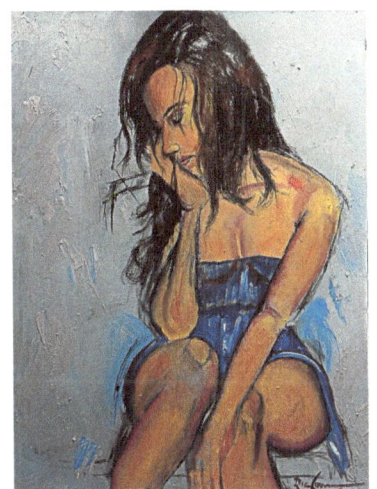

Sad Girl
(2017) Pastel Painting

Ric Conn

ricconn.com

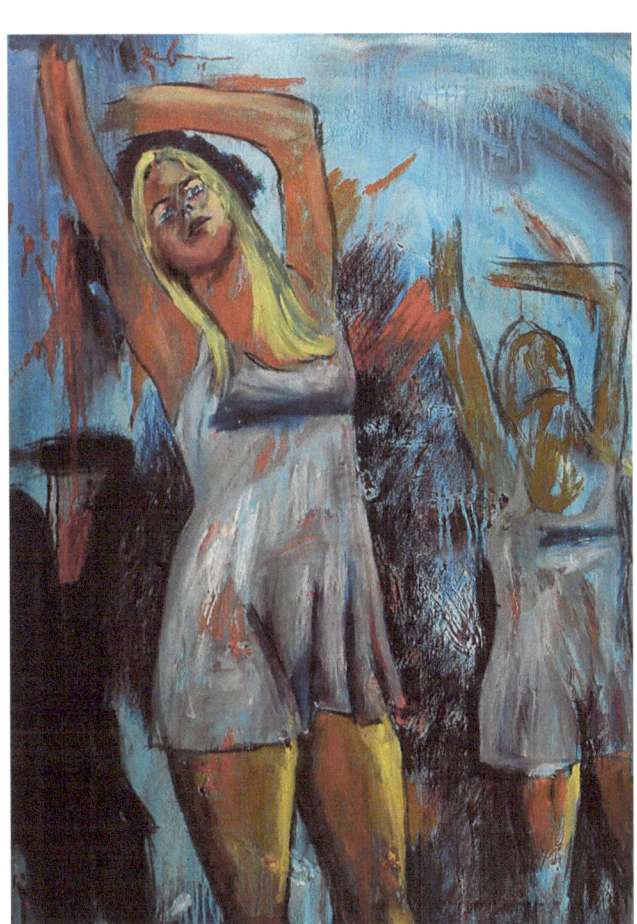

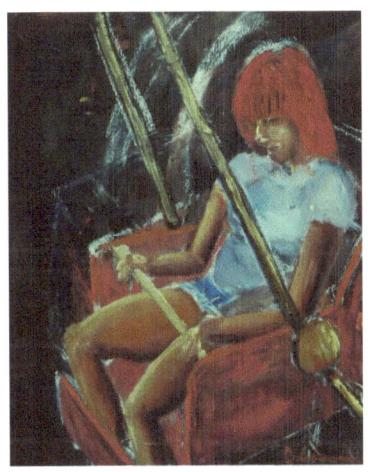

Ferris Wheel
(2017) Pastel Painting

Shadow Dancer
(2017) Pastel Painting

Cambridge artist Maureen Farrell also takes an expressionistic approach to her stories. Currently, she makes collages depicting women walking singly or in groups. "It's all coming out of my heart and my head, and where I've been before. And, it's evolving. I'm excited to see where it's going to go. I've been told by people that it's very emotional. I've come to realize that a lot of the figures actually are me at different stages of my life. There is something deep inside of me that is coming out. And, I am just going with it. I'm not forcing anything. I am just letting it happen."

Megan Burak, a recent graduate of Salisbury University from Berlin, Maryland, tells a similar story with her stunning self-portraits. Using photo-realism, she explores ideas about things like privacy and relationships. Megan does not want to spoon feed the viewer a story in her paintings. "I want people to not just look at it and leave. I want people to look at it and say: What is she trying to say with this?"

One story teller who is perhaps the preeminent Impressionist painter on Delmarva, is Patrick Henry who is also from Berlin. He is prolific, painting a variety of subjects including rural Delmarva, and scenes from his travels. He too wants viewers to leave thinking about what they have just seen. One of Patrick's recent paintings was based on an old photograph his mother took when she was a local Head Start coordinator. With his beautiful strokes in gentle hues he captures a moment of childhood fun on a playground. Patrick expects this scene will leave people musing just as he has: "These children; three, four, or five years old; are at the height of promise. This image was taken some thirty years ago. I wonder: Where are they now? I wonder. Each one of them have their own body language. This one has a security blanket. And I wonder about this one little white boy, in a sea of black faces. Where does he stand with race relations now?"

Artists both create and preserve a region's cultural heritage and the story of its people. Delmarva's storyteller artists demonstrate that within each of us is a story waiting to be told if only we can find the courage and the means to do so.

Maureen Farrell

maureensfarrell.com

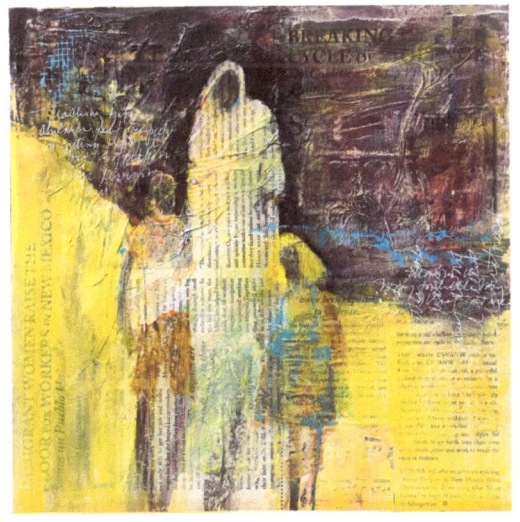

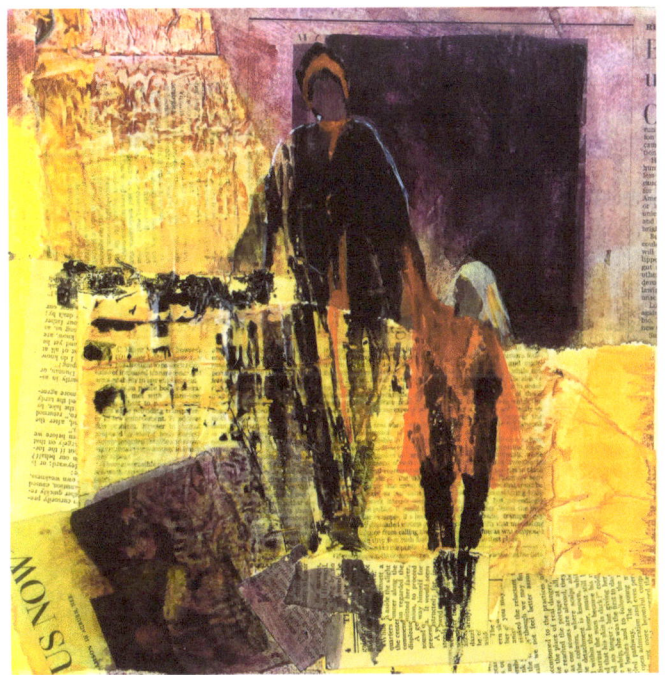

Us
(2015) Mixed Media / Collage

Breaking the Cycle
(2016) Mixed Media / Collage

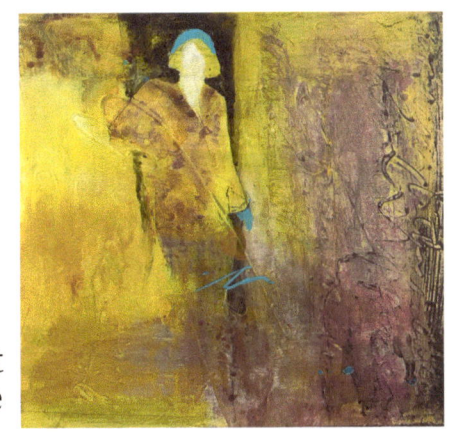

Blue Hat
(2017) Mixed Media / Collage

Megan Burak

meganburak.com

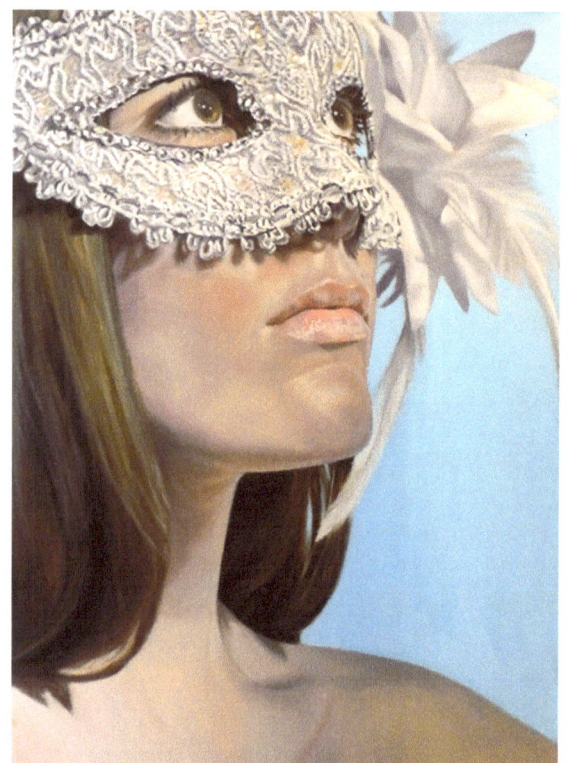

I Need You To See
(2015) Oil on canvas

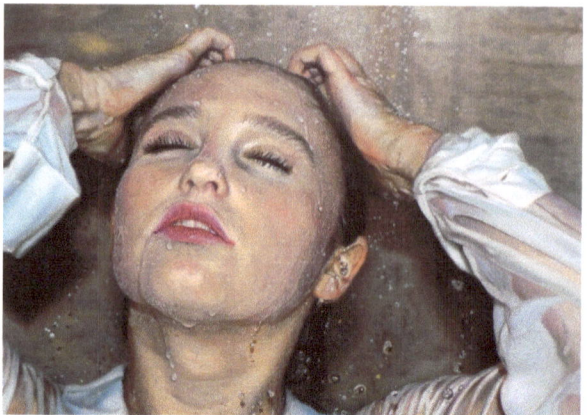

Soaked
(2015) Oil on canvas

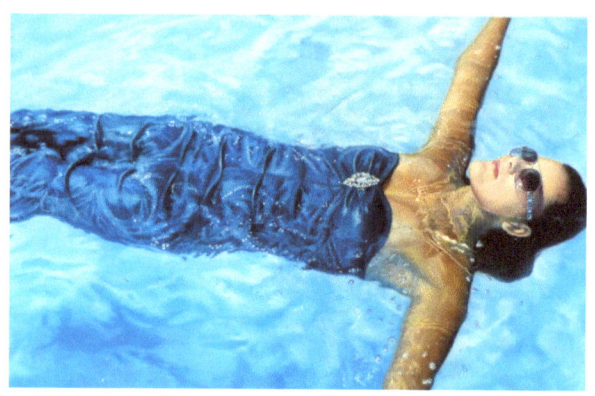

After Prom
(2015) Oil on canvas

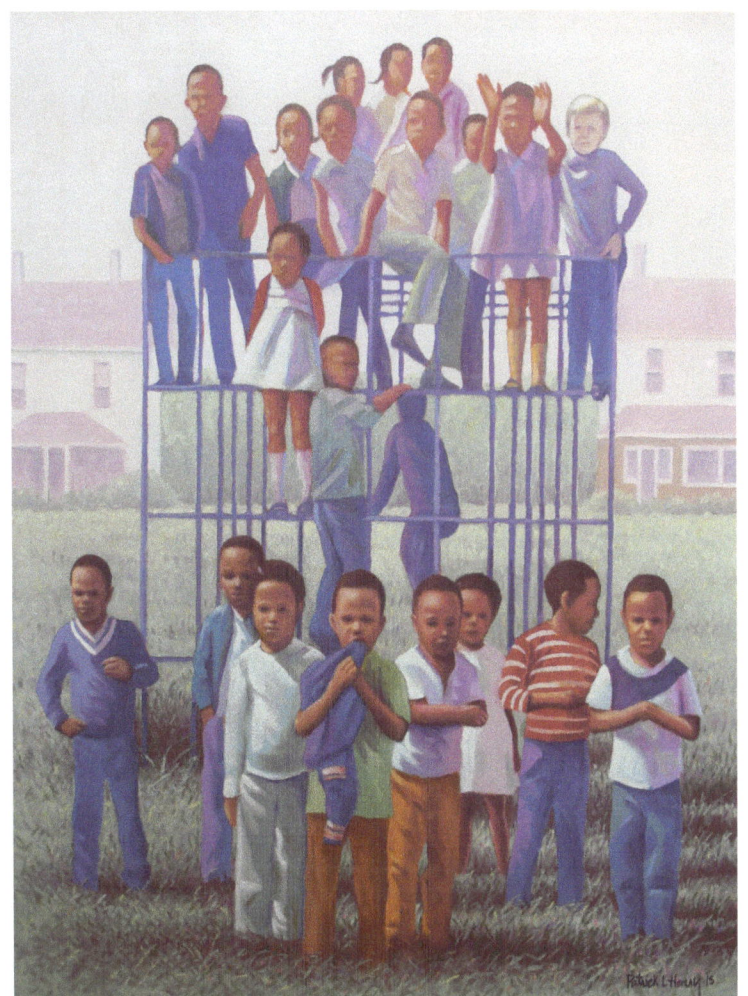

I Wonder
(2015) Oil on canvas

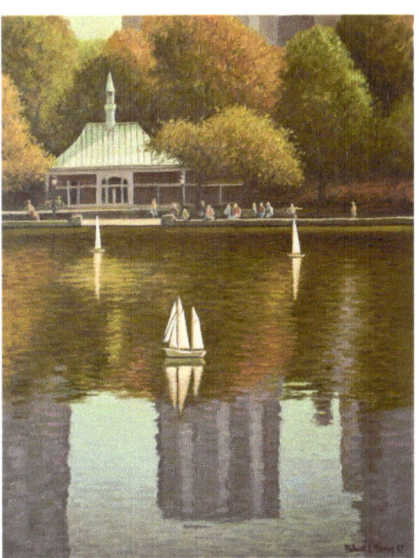

Central Park -
Saturday Morning
(2017) Oil on canvas

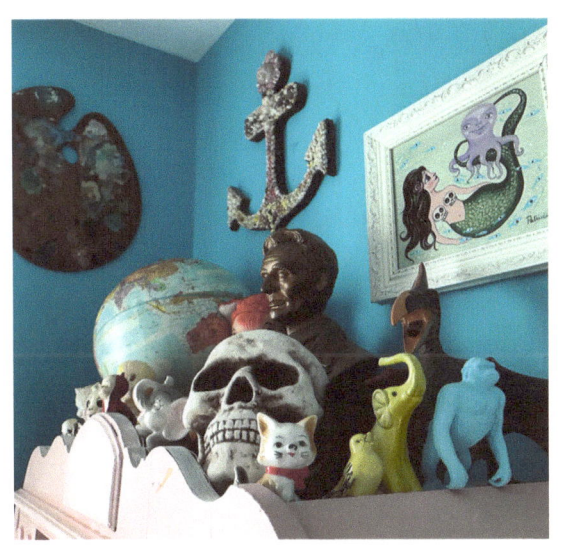
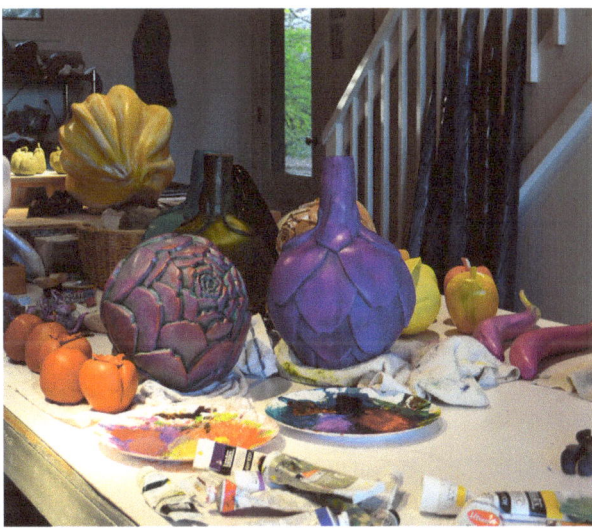
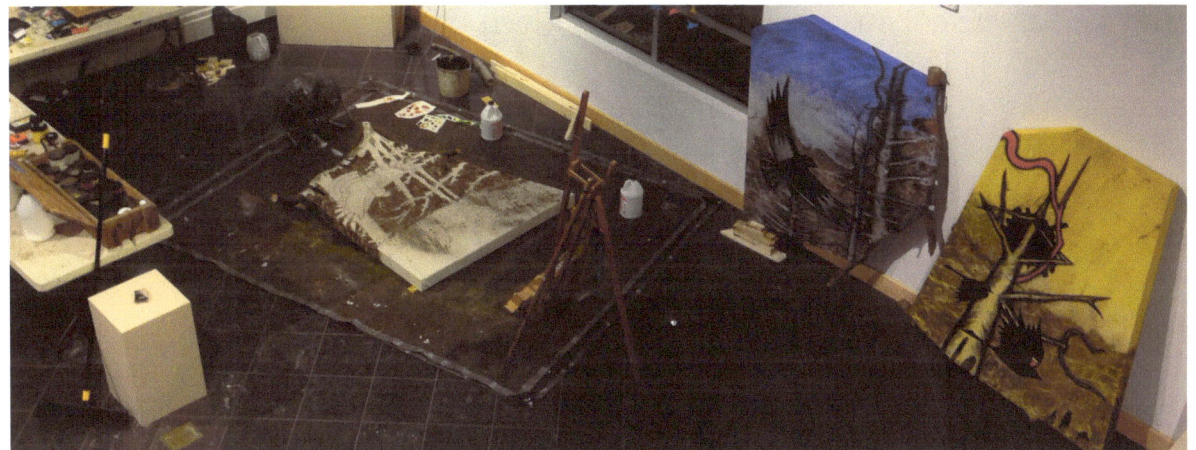

Fearless Imaginations

Many of Delmarva's artists are called to go beyond usual expectations: to not only tell their own stories but to do it in their own way. They commit to an idea and then produce a work of art regardless of whether it may be considered weird or even dangerous. Challenging preconceived notions, making the audience think or feel something, these require unfettered creativity. Whether you see it in the artists' subject matter or their unconventional approach to materials, there is no shortage of fearless imaginations here on Delmarva.

Milton artist Aurelio Grisanty has built a successful business designing stylish crisp graphic Art Deco inspired travel posters. His equally beautiful fine art paintings are more expressionistic. He paints standing at a very large table which is covered with a blank white canvas. He works on a variety of projects allowing any paint that drips or spills on to the cloth to become a part of his next work. By the end of about three months, that canvas is beautifully stained. He begins working into the lovely random marks with different images and lines from which compositions emerge. Sometimes he uses the whole sheet. Other times he cuts it into smaller pieces. Aurelio stretches these canvases onto frames and then adds figurative and design elements. Each work is built on the effects of other paintings and becomes a reflection of not only his other work, but a sort of journal entry recording his state of mind at the time of its creation.

Rob Brownlee-Tomasso also takes an unusual approach to his materials. For him it is all about breaking the usual conventions of art. Rob works from photos he has taken of birds, landscapes, and buildings, among other things. Those images are not all that he brings back to his studio in Denton, Maryland. Wherever he collects an image he also gathers up some dirt or sand to use as texture in his paintings. This imbues the work physically with the spirit of the place he is portraying. He treats his subject matter to a graphic sensibility with black outlines and high contrast colors. He breaks away from standard art presentation stretching his canvases asymmetrically sometimes on tree branches. His innovative strategy

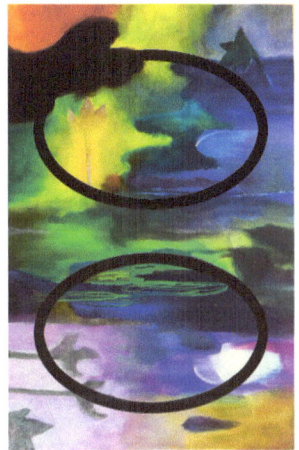

Lake
(2015) Mixed Media
oil on canvas

The Two Lakes
(2015) Mixed Media
oil on canvas

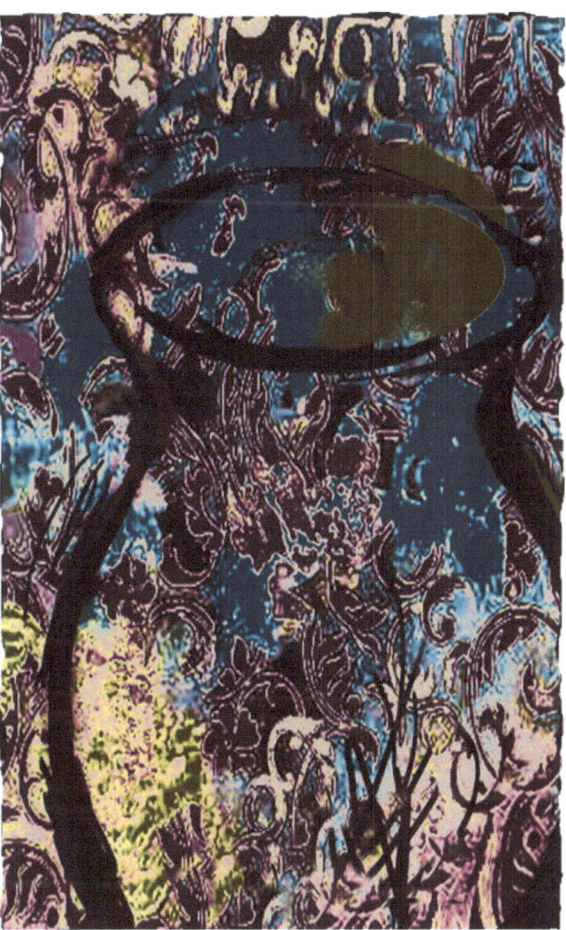

Vase
(2015) Mixed Media oil on canvas

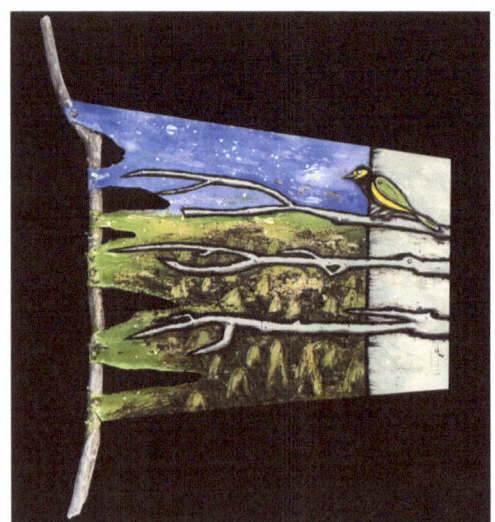

The Woods #2
(2016) Acrylic and earth on canvas

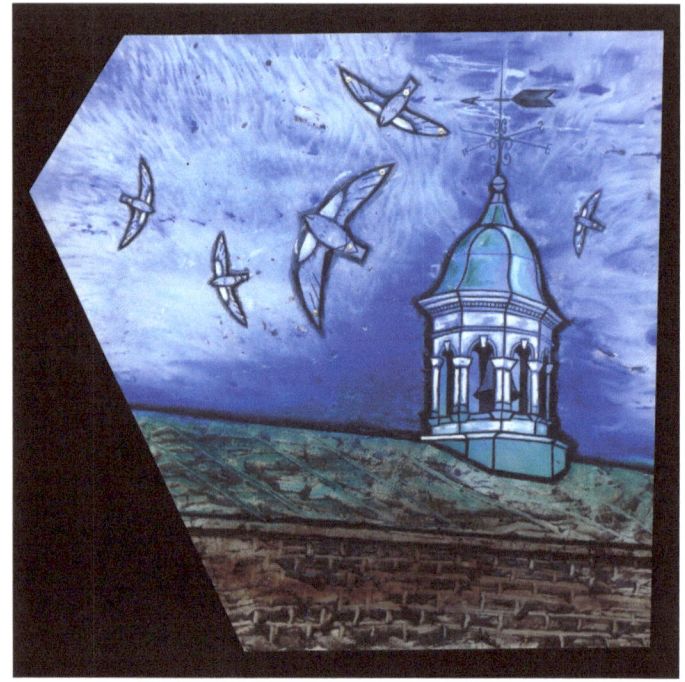

Chimney Swifts
(2016) Acrylic and earth on canvas

Hooded Warbler
(2017) Acrylic and earth on canvas

results in dramatic imagery that leaves a strong impression.

Susan Holt, of Salisbury, Maryland, breaks out even further from traditional art supplies to create thought provoking art installations, large three-dimensional works of art which are meant to be immersive interactive experiences for the viewer. Here on Delmarva, installations are not the most a common form of art in part because it is not easy to find funding for them and they usually take a team of people to construct. With a few volunteers Susan created a large weaving of cloth strips each containing phrases written on them from interviews with Salisbury residents about their memories of the town. This collaborative sculpture has been shown several times and it has its own Facebook page where people continue to share memories. Another piece by Susan was influenced by a trip she led for students to the Venice Biennale in Italy. It was a life size shear fabric portico which she built for a faculty art show at Salisbury University. The light airy material transformed the space with an evocative dreamy magic.

Jan Kirsh, a sculptor and landscape designer from Talbot County Maryland, also knows how to cast an enchanted spell with her work. She says fun is really important in the garden and in art. Her pieces begin in clay and plaster using traditional tools that have been around for centuries. Then Jan jumps ahead to a very modern technique: 3-D computer modeling. Scanning her hand made originals, she can then cast any size: from jewelry-sized pieces like a gold onion she wears on a chain around her neck, to larger pieces like a giant pear she created for the garden at the Bartlett Pear Inn in Easton. Some of Jan's works are produced in bronze, and others are cast in resin then finished with automobile body paint giving them a durable, colorful, and lustrous sheen. Her large voluptuous fruits and vegetables have a great sense of sensual whimsy. Even without knowing the process she uses, they make bold colorful statements.

Susan Holt

delmarvaschoolofart.info/holt

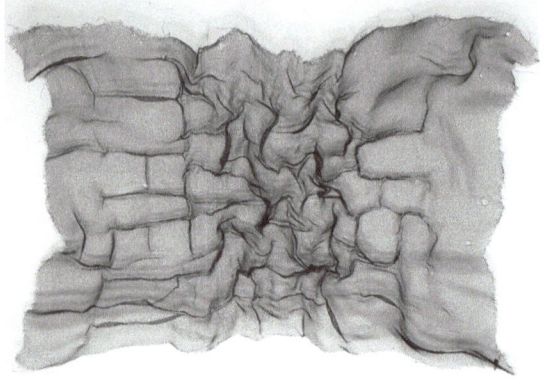

Us/Them
(2015) Screening

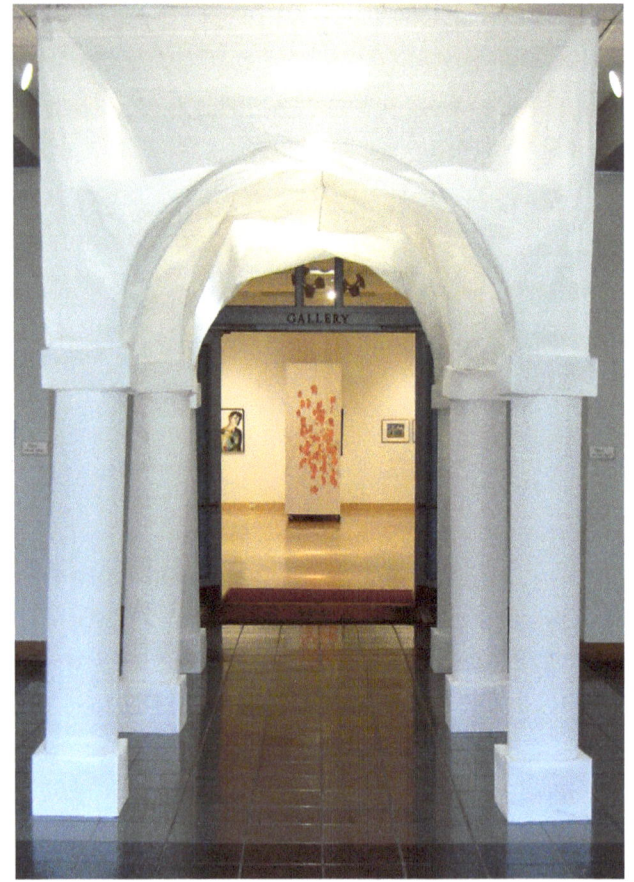

Memories of Bologna
(2013) Installation

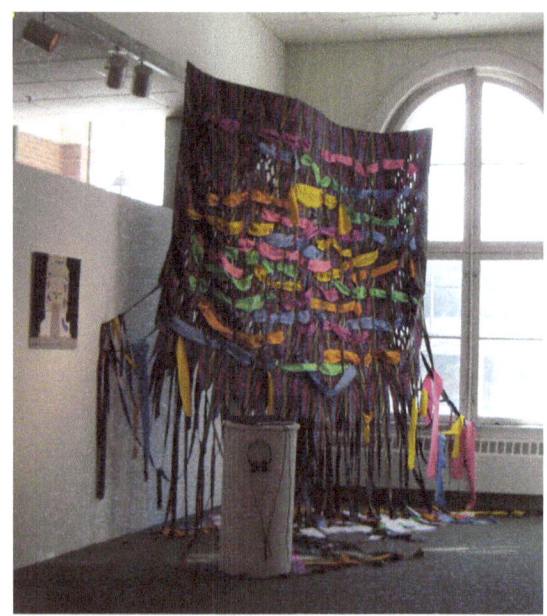

Memories of Downtown
(2010-ongoing) Installation

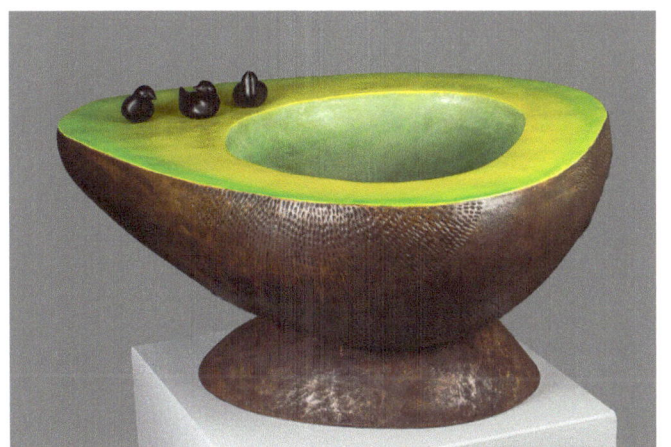

Avocado Half
(2014) Fiberglass

Jan Kirsh

jankirshstudio.com

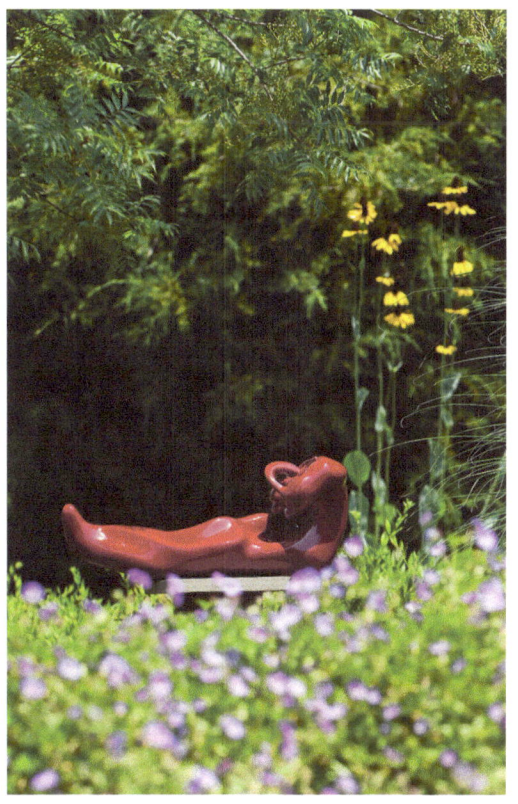

Mid Century Modern Screen
(2013) Corten Steel

Chile Pepper
(2008) Cast Resin

For another sculptor, Maurice Spector of Pungoteague Virginia, every new piece is a unique creative adventure. He says he does not know where his inspiration comes from, except perhaps from his heart. His style cannot be completely tied down to one thing though many of his works are smooth round monolithic animals and humans of carved stone or cast metal. Some are small and others are large. He also carves in wood. Mo's joy for life and art is infectious. If you attend the annual November artist studio tour on the Eastern Shore of Virginia which includes a stop at his historic farm, you will be treated to a menagerie of his sculptures and graphic paintings. Other artists also set up tents there to show their wares. They roast oysters and serve wine and beer. The hospitality and creativity on display make it one of the most popular stops on the tour.

For Isabel Umanzor, a native of Chile, creative expression comes in the form of both music and painting. She grew up during the time of the Pinochet dictatorship when music was central to the spirit of rebellion. She joined a group of folk singers when she was just eleven. Since moving to Delaware as an adult, her day job has been as a Spanish teacher. Her night job was to perform her own songs, along with popular covers, guitar in hand at local pubs. Isabel is also a visual artist. Her paintings are moody and expressionistic. She calls them "graphic dreaming". Both painting and songwriting have helped her to deal with the emotional impact of moving to a new country, what she left behind, and her hopes for social change:

"If with the ears of a child you capture the sound, I maybe could sing
for those who gave their lives fighting for something that always they dreamed…"
- from the song Childish World by Isabel Umanzor (Translated from Spanish)

Bill Wright uses his imagination as they say on Star Trek "to explore strange new worlds… to boldly go where no man has gone before." Bill is a science fiction and fantasy artist. He has a degree in biology which provides him with a scientific eye for accuracy and plausibility in his life like compositions. Using images of space freely

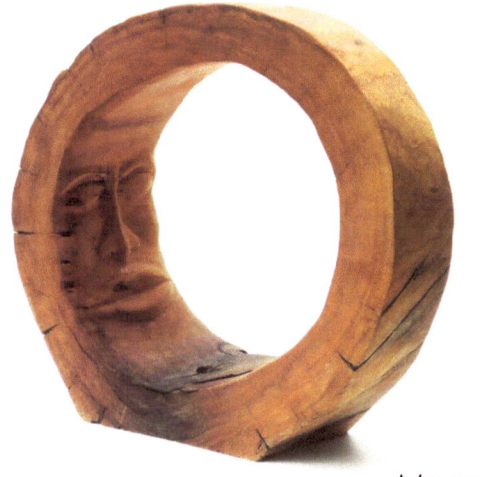

Dancing Horse
(2017) Bronze

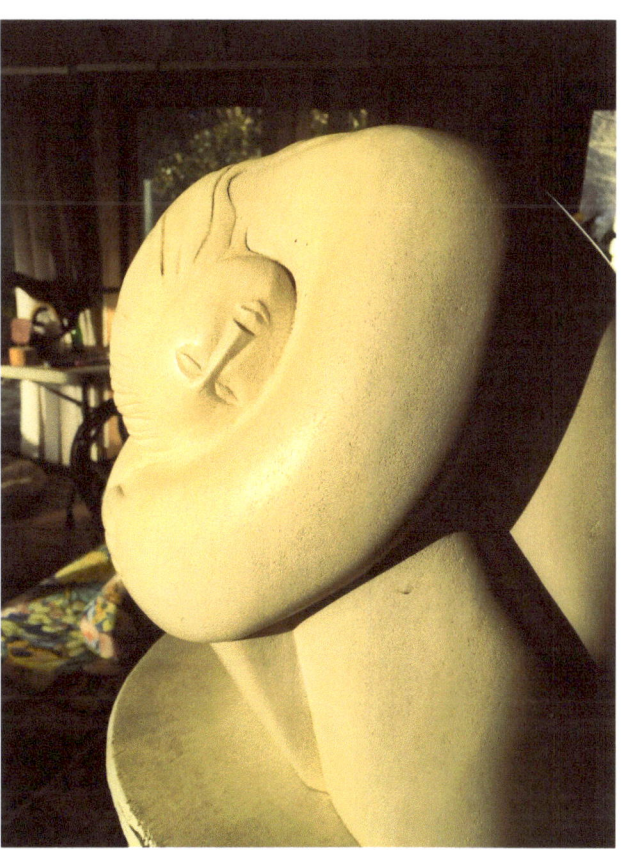

Moon
(2016) Wood

Woman In Wave
(2011) Limestone

Isabel Umanzor

facebook.com/isabeluf

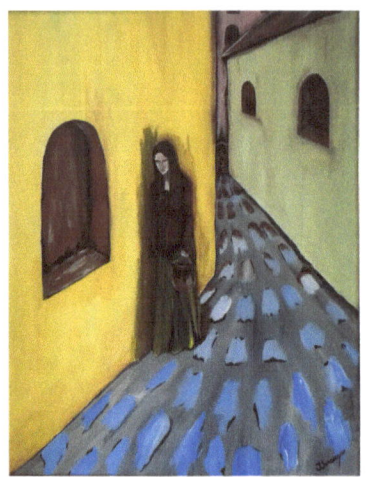

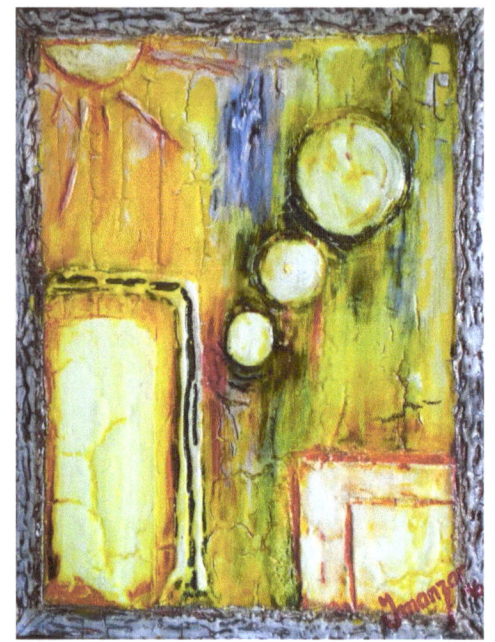

Dime
(2005) Acrylic

Tres Lunas
(2016) Acrylic

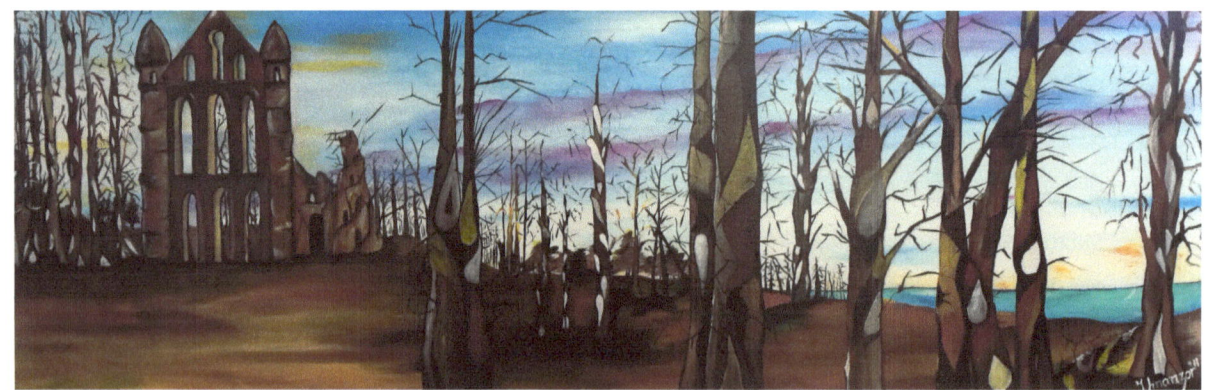

Ruinas
(2009) Acrylic

40

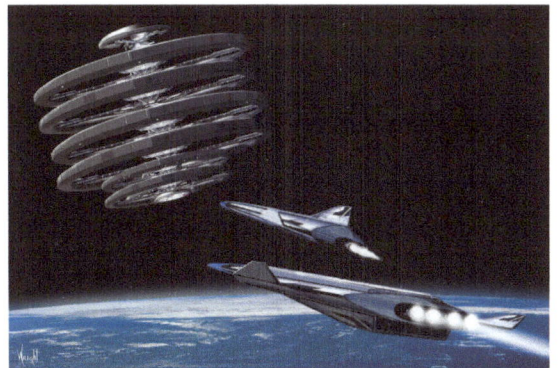

Two Stage Orbit
(2016) Digital Painting

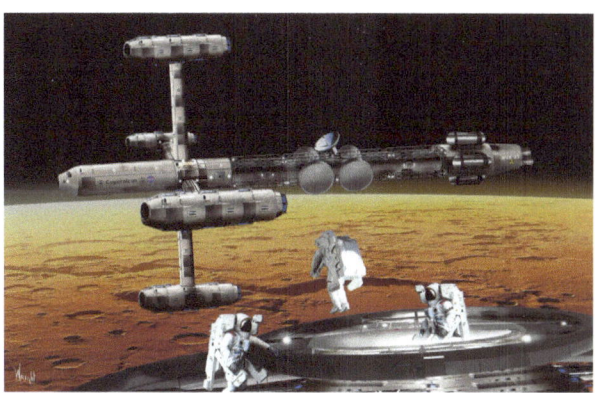

Mars EVA
(2016) Digital Painting

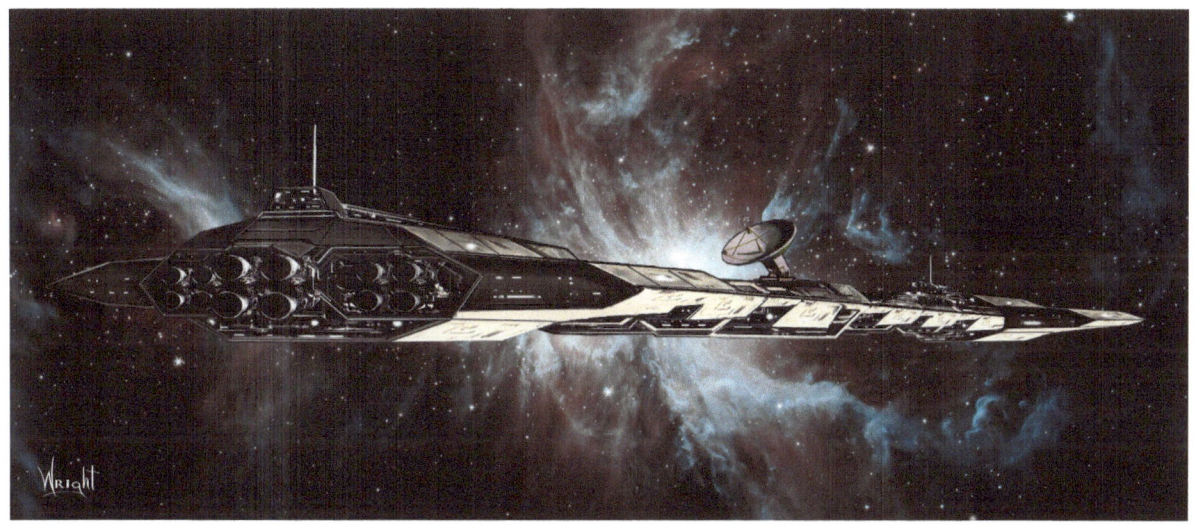

Starship
(2016) Digital Painting

provided by NASA, his digital and acrylic paintings imagine space travel with photographic clarity. He has created illustrations for articles written by the likes of astronaut Buzz Aldrin for the Planetary Society. His work is not only inspired by real life space travel, but it has the beauty and power to inspire future exploration of this galaxy and beyond.

Painter Helene English has her imagination planted firmly here on earth. She also begins with photographs, saying she says she does not like to "make things up in her head". She works from the reality she observes and then projects her own abstraction and stylization on to her subjects. Helene lives on the Wicomico River. This provides ample inspiration, especially the frequent traffic of big tug boats which seem to dwarf the little stream they travel on. Other topics which she paints include carousel animals and humorous dog scenes, which she does purely for fun. Those dog paintings are perhaps her most popular. They are a witty commentary on how human personalities are displayed by their canines and sometimes vice-versa.

Berlin artist Patti Backer takes the real world and reimagines it completely with her fun and imaginative work. She paints large eyed-creatures and fantastical scenes on wood, old furniture, and canvas. She also produces a variety of ornaments and greeting cards. Her compositions have the feel of children's books with bright graphic colors. But, they have a twist. Sometimes it is the sculls in the images and sometimes it is creatures looking out at you with a sort of playful menace. She describes her art as "a mix of folk and lowbrow… sweet and sinister." Patti has an intuitive creative process which leads to a prolific production schedule of wonderfully weird and whimsical art.

A very fertile imagination is also at the heart of Dana Simson's work. She says that when she is beginning a project she pulls ideas from many sources and places them "in a bowl and mixes them all up". Dana is a painter, a potter, a jewelry

Helene English
ugallery.com/helene-english

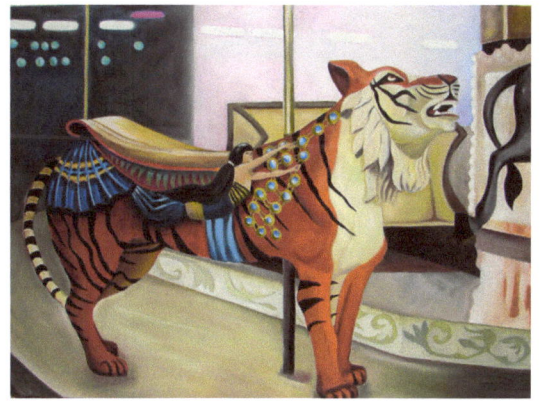

Ocean City Carousel
(2006) Oil on canvas

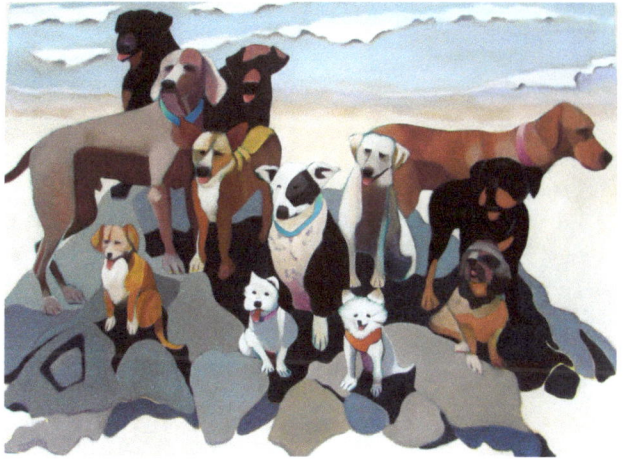

One Dozen Dogs
(2015) Oil on canvas

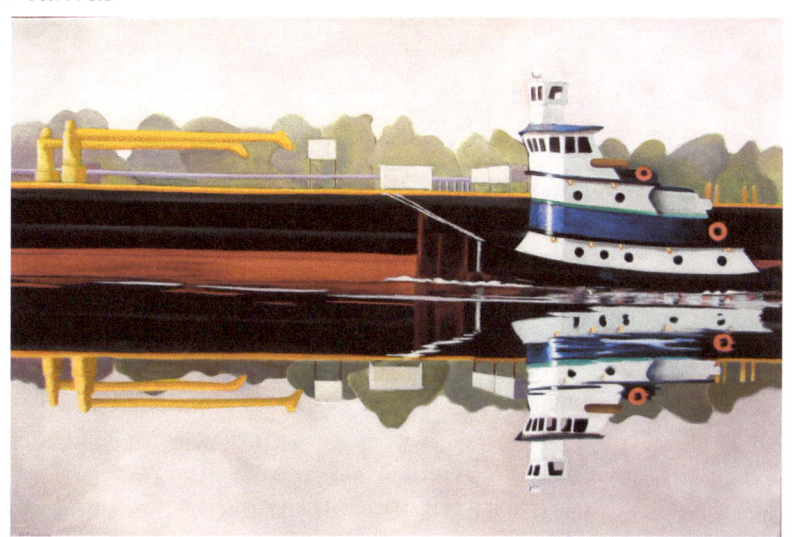

Double Skin
(2012) Oil on canvas

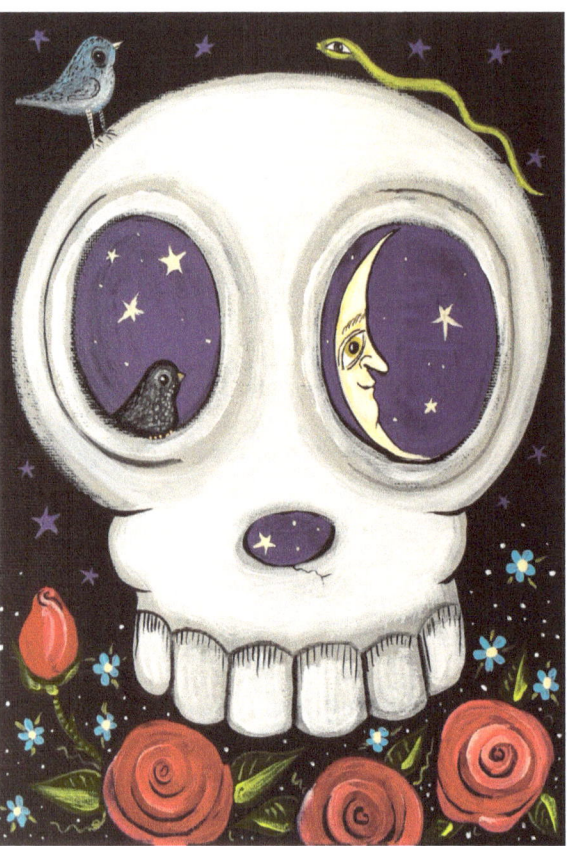

Chicken Butt
(2015) Acrylic on canvas

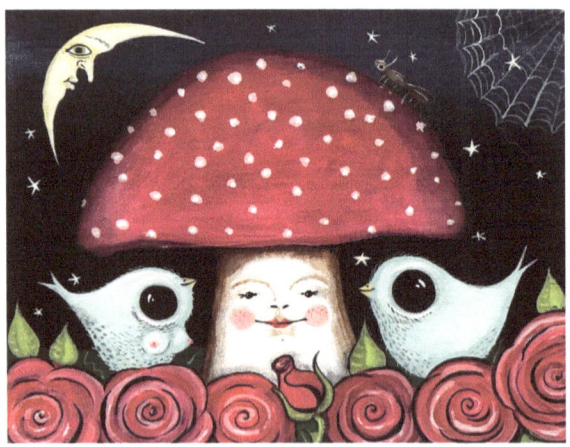

Mushroom The Matchmaker
(2017) Acrylic on canvas

Garden Skull
(2016) Acrylic on canvas

Dana Simson

danasimson.com

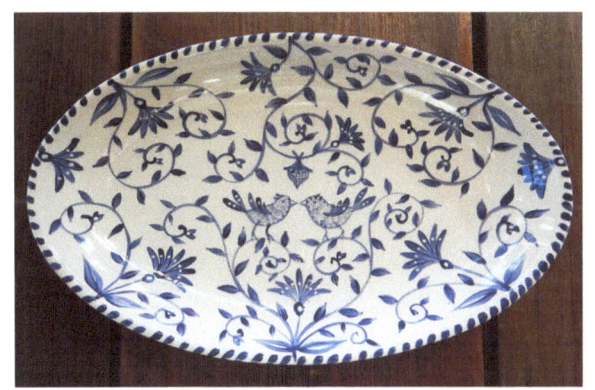

Wishing You Happy Nest
(2016) Painted Platter

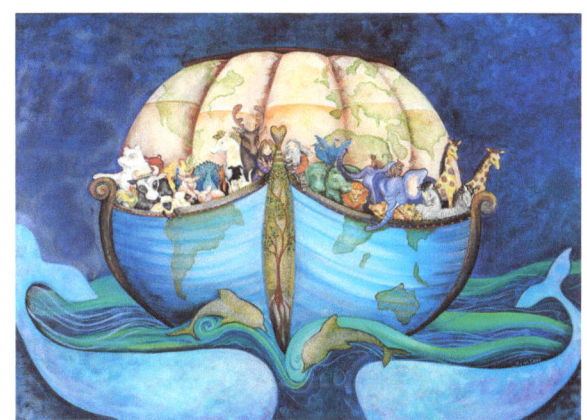

Earthark
(2008) Oils

Dolly Summer's End
(2015) Oils

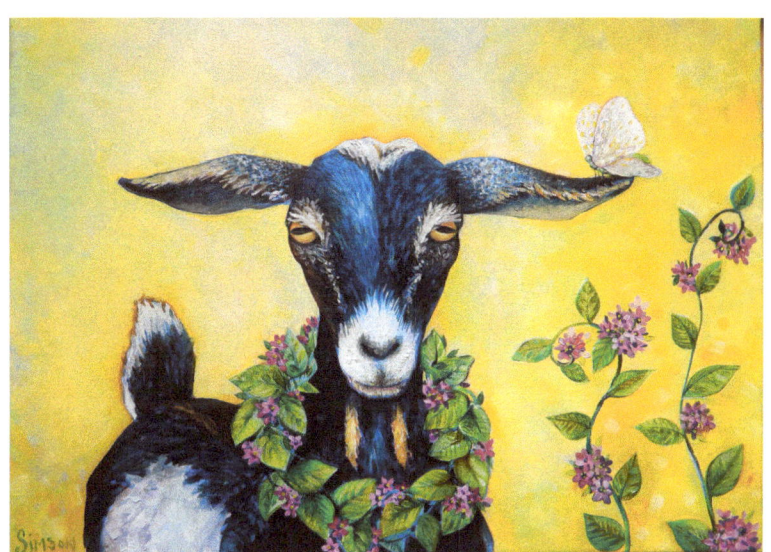

maker, and an author of children's books and political satire. Her gallery Chesapeake East in Salisbury is filled with colorful handmade artwork and dishware, among other things. Across all these mediums you can see Dana's light-hearted style and sense of humor. Dana calls herself an illustrator. She says she wants people to insert themselves into her art and interact with it. Indeed, she could easily have been in the storytellers' chapter of this book.

One thing all the artists in this chapter have in common is that they are all very prolific. The ideas fill their minds and art pours out. Jack Knight is a good example. He paints large canvases with geometric shapes and patterns in brilliant sometimes neon colors. He also makes sculptural assemblages from found objects painted with the same approach as his two-dimensional work. His style is reminiscent of 1960's pop art. All through Jack's career working for the railroad he continued to make art in his spare time. Now that he is retired and living in lower Delaware Jack says that his art has become a fulltime job that doesn't feel like work at all.

Art has always been Snow Hill artist Paul Volker's fulltime job. He left art school when he was too busy to attend class because he was already "doing actual art jobs for people". He has done thousands of small single panel cartoon paintings mostly of animal jokes. He uses unconventional materials to create his paintings and bas reliefs: house paint and recycled paper pulp. Paul enjoys experimenting with his materials, using them in unexpected ways.

Paul wants to challenge the viewer to think beyond the ordinary. "In the world today, we're getting all our information on these glass screens. And, we're losing that sort of textural quality to our experience. And so, I want to create artwork that you can feel the texture with your eyes. You can feel some depth. It's not just something behind glass."

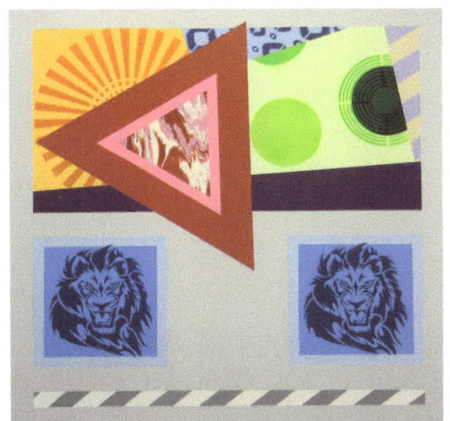

Sunnyside Series #24
(2017) Oil and acrylic on canvas

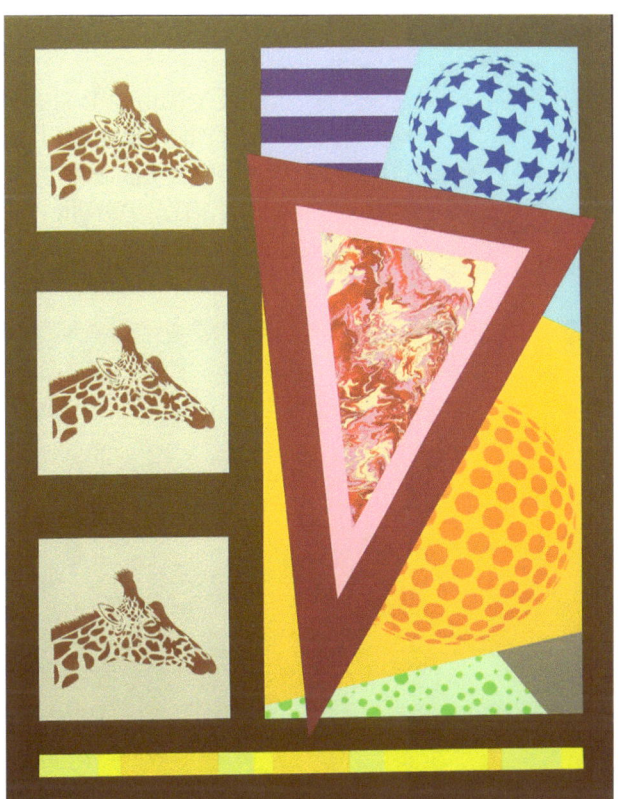

Sunnyside Series #11
(2017) Oil and acrylic on canvas

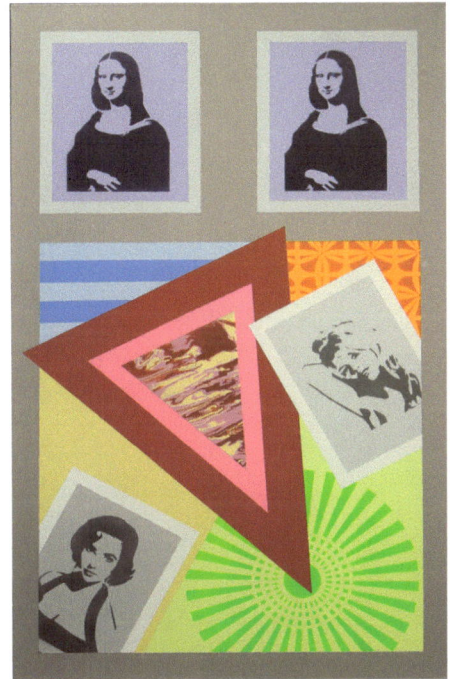

Sunnyside Series #19
(2017) Oil and acrylic on canvas

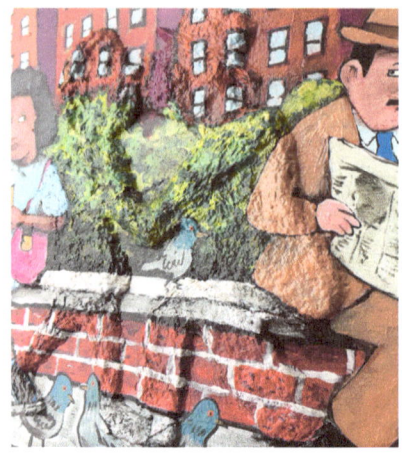

Paul Volker

volkerworld.com

Detail Left: side view
Full painting below
Perfect strangers imagine the pigeons don't exist
(2017) Acrylic house paint, wood, recycled paper pulp

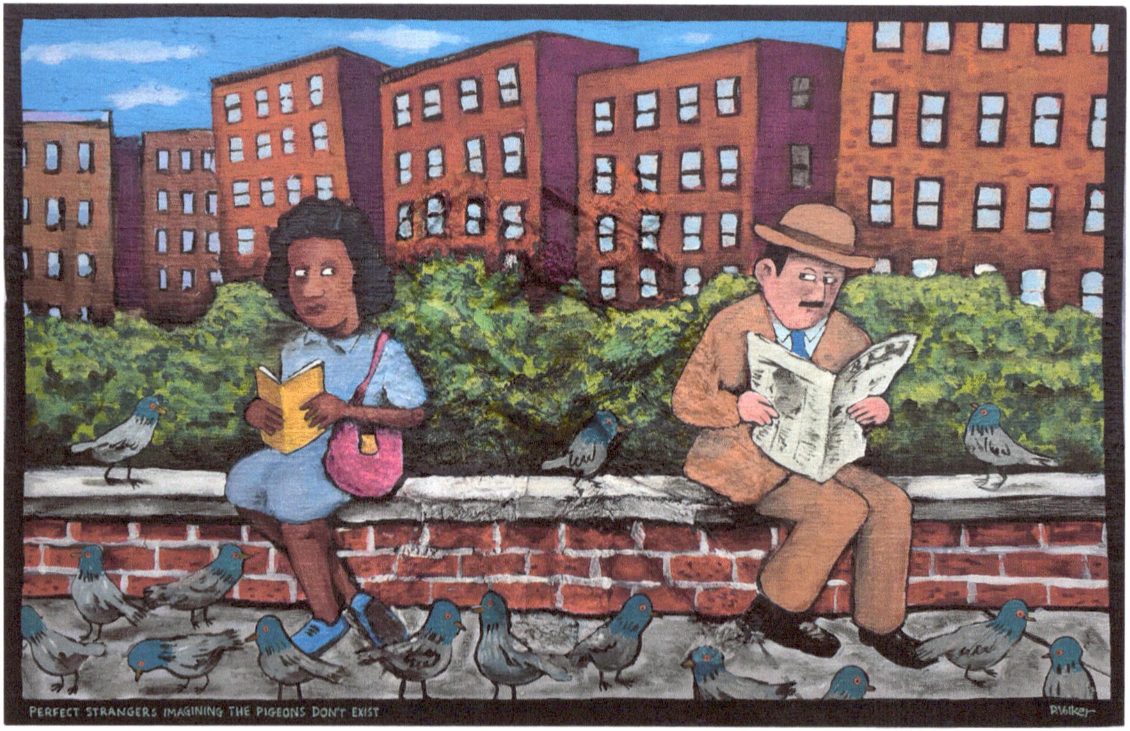

PERFECT STRANGERS IMAGINING THE PIGEONS DON'T EXIST

With all that technology has to offer, life would be much poorer without hand crafted art that we can actually hold in our hands or walk up to and around. One cannot replace the other. It is the artist's job to tell our untold stories, to notice what we have ignored, to remember what we have forgotten, and to imagine what we have not yet dreamed of. How fortunate we are that Delmarva is the perfect place for these artists to use their fearless imaginations to help us see what we are missing.

Opposite page images:
Kirk McBride
Studio Interior
(2017) Digital Photograph

Dana Kester-McCabe
Glassblower At The Glory Hole
(2012) Digital Photograph

Late Day Island
(2016) Digital Photograph
Courtesy of Michele Green

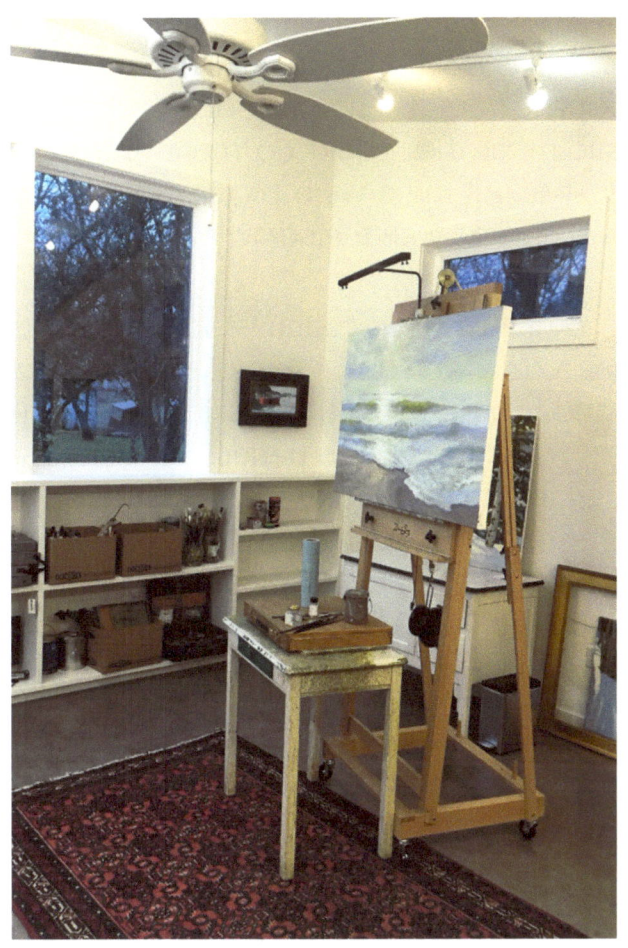
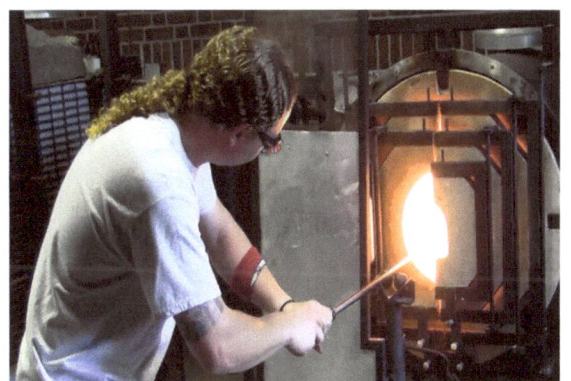
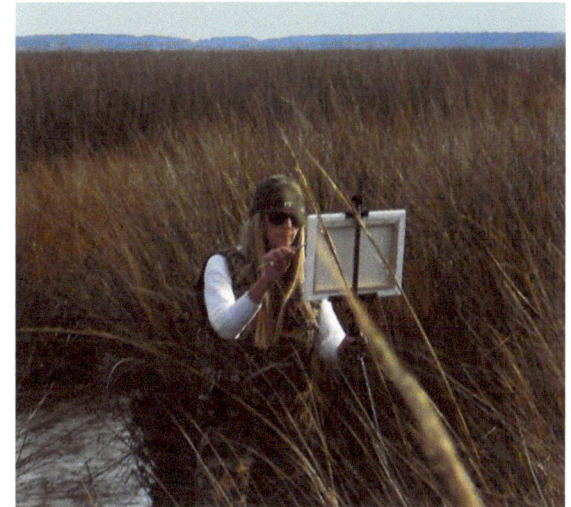

The Freedom of Discipline

Artists are often portrayed as lazy self-indulgent daydreamers. This could not be farther from the reality of the people I met on my interviews. They may be dreamers but they are very hard workers. I once did a series of stories with three artists who were also skateboarders. The reputation of skaters is similarly inaccurate. These three men had learned a lifelong habit of self-discipline from skating: practicing their moves over and over again until they were satisfied that they could do more and more challenging tricks with greater and greater style. All three were prolific artists, who when not working on larger pieces filled sketchbooks with their drawings.

This is also true for Berlin painter Lynne Lockhart who has countless volumes of her drawings. Like a competitive athlete she has a daily workout. In pencil, she practices animal anatomy studying how the bones and muscles work under skin and fur. She says she uses plein air landscape painting as "cross training" to perfect her style. The results are masterful Impressionist paintings with brush strokes that not only look effortless, but whose subjects look as if they could jump off the surface and come alive. Her dogs and farm animals are playful and often funny. With genuine humility, she credits the masters: "They have all helped me. Long dead artists are still helping me." She says that the key for her is her practice of daily drawing and the "miles and miles of canvas" she has painted that make each new work appear fresh and spontaneous.

For many artists drawing is ingrained in their daily routine but it is not something to be shared with anyone. A drawing can, however, stand on its own as a finished work of art. Milton Delaware artist, Barbara Warden, turned to drawing as her primary medium having previously concentrated on the fiber arts, specifically quilting. Her expressionistic drawings are rich with texture and movement. Her daily discipline became a year-long series documenting her reactions to her favorite hiking trails in Montana. Each day she assigned herself the task of doing one finished work of art using one word to drive the feelings she was expressing. The

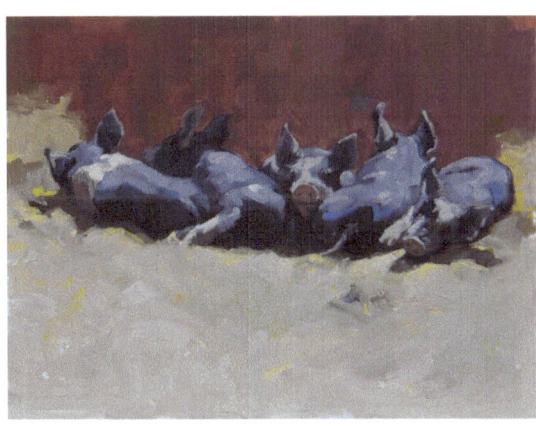

Hay For Breakfast
(2016) Oils

Warmer Barn
(2017) Oils

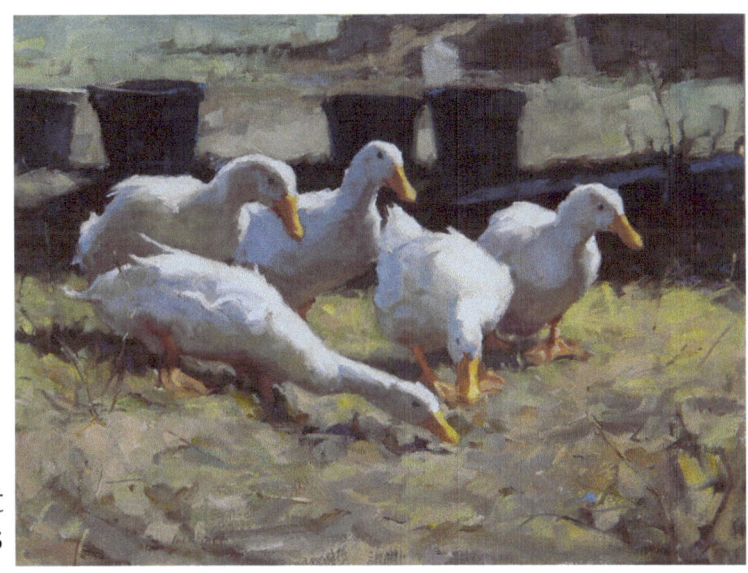

Snail Hunt
(2017) Oils

Barbara Warden

firetalkarts.com

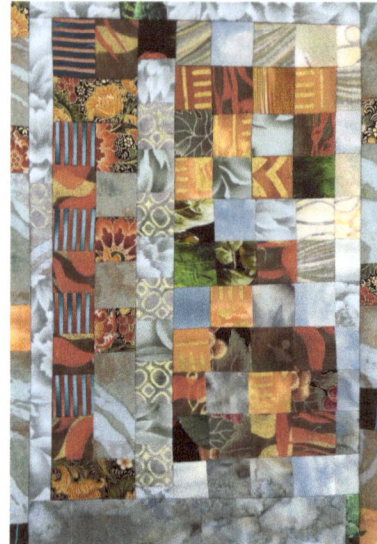

Redstone
(2016) Quilt (Fiber)

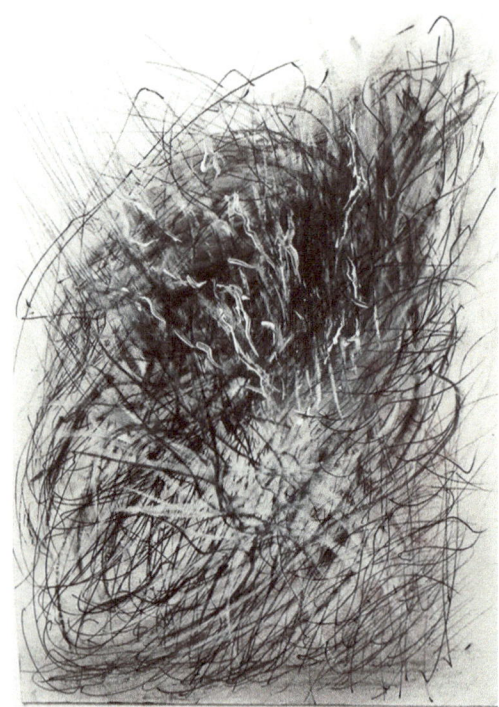

Smoke
(2015) Ink, conte crayon, acrylic
enamel on paper

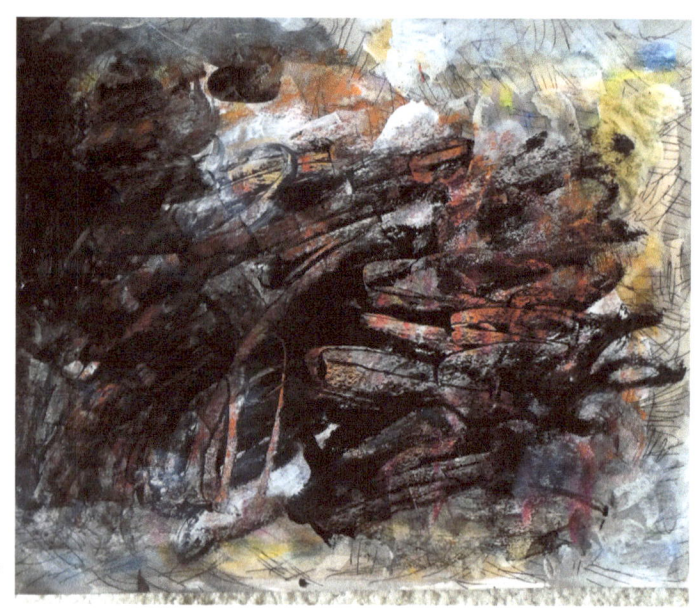

Wind
(2016) Graphite, ink, acrylic on paper

first word was: stone. Then came ice, then rain, wind, and then restless ground. She continued to do drawings about these words and many more. She describes her process this way: "I start with a gesture and I end up with a resolution, I think. Set it aside, and go on to the next one." Barbara's endeavors culminated in a series of almost four hundred abstract expressionist drawings which were featured in a solo show at the Biggs Museum in Dover, Delaware.

The raw power and beauty of nature is also the subject matter of plein air painter Michele Green whose studio is the wide-open marshes of Somerset County, Maryland. Her daily year-round almost-all-weather discipline requires not only physical strength but tough tenacity. Accompanied only by canine companions, often dressed in hip-boot waders, she pulls her supplies on a sled from her truck or boat to her painting sites. There are many distractions that make it hard to focus: bugs, wind, and even the wider view of the landscape. Sometimes the environment controls her. "Sometimes it wins." Michele says. A storm can come up or one of her dogs might scare a skunk making it necessary for her to make a hasty retreat. Michele describes her soft dreamy style as a mix between impressionism and abstraction. She says it has taken practice, practice, practice, and a long time to reach the point of creative maturity where she no longer throws her paintings in the bushes on her way home.

Outdoor experiences including plein air painting are also central to Snow Hill artist Scot Dolby's creative process. Scot is well known for his paintings of freshwater fish and landscapes. He is a fly fisher who paints as much as he is a painter who loves fly fishing. He says that fly fishing is almost a meditative practice, during which he gets some of his best ideas for paintings. His fishing passion has taken him to some of the country's great rivers where he will sometimes live out doors for almost a month fishing, sketching, and taking photographs. Scot says this helps him to look at the world from the outside in rather than the inside out. There

Michele Green

michelegreen.net

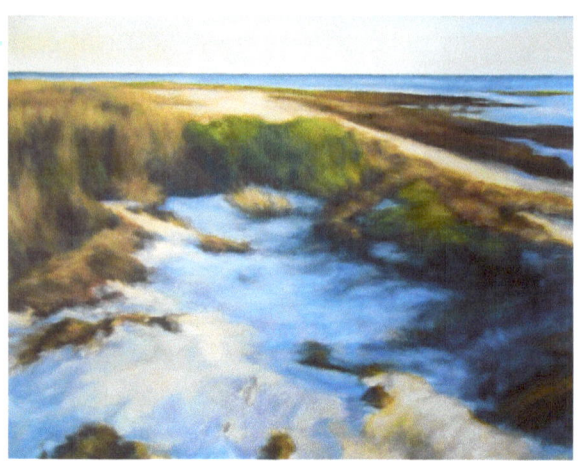

Late Day Island
(2016) Oil on canvas

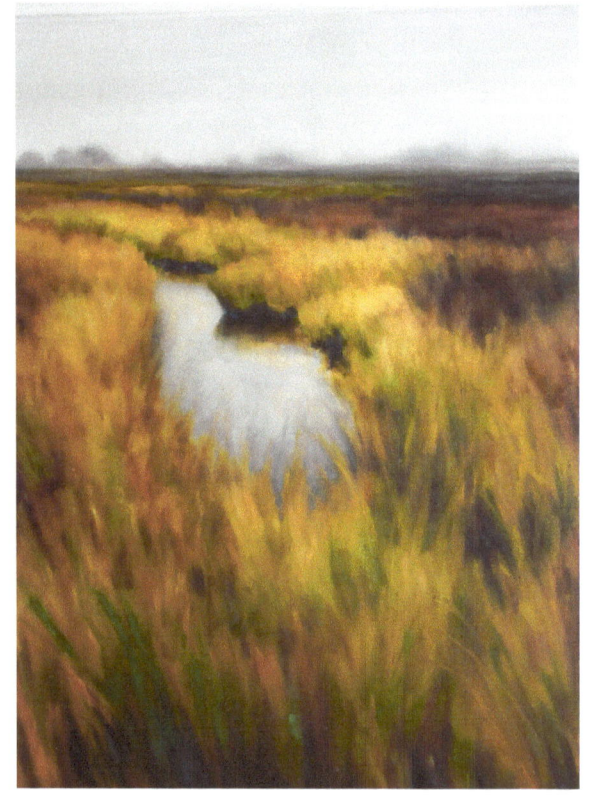

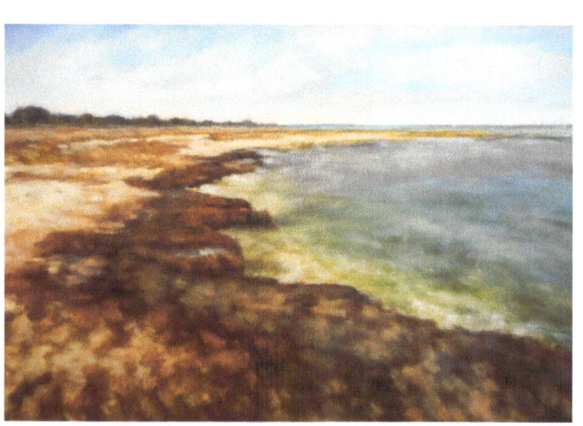

Gold Marsh
(2016) Oil on canvas

Sea Drift
(2016) Oil on canvas

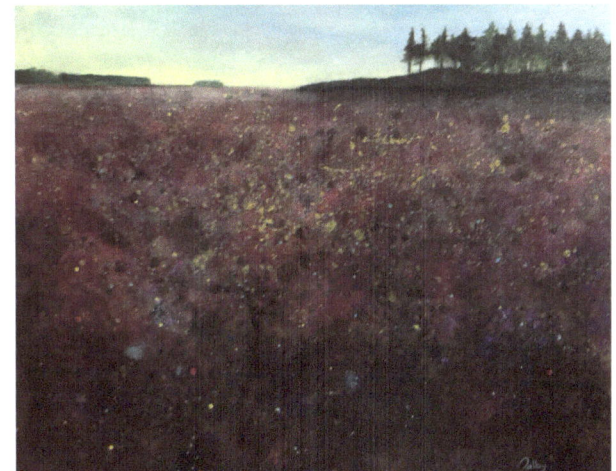

On The Creek
(2016) Acrylic

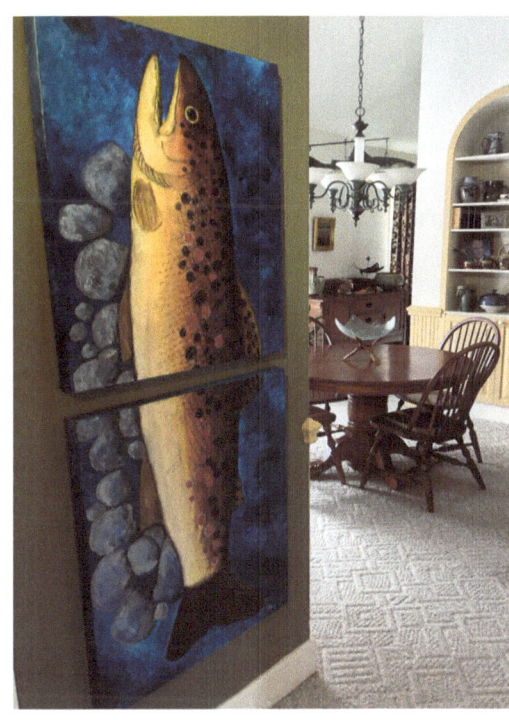

Beaverhead Brown Diptych
(2000) Acrylic

North
(2007) Acrylic

is also a correlation between the trained dancelike moves of fly-fishing and Scot's free and easy painting style that is the result of several years of experimentation and practice.

For printmaker Erick Sahler, artistic discipline happens in his studio. His chosen form of printmaking is serigraphy (silkscreen printing). This requires detailed technical expertise. Mastery of this medium is achieved only through rigorous discipline. Each color is printed separately, and details must match up in order to create his clean graphic lines. Erick's dedication to fine craftsmanship is rewarded with beautiful fine art prints. It is interesting how the deliberate process he uses to execute his prints contrasts with his lighthearted approach to subject matter. One of his series, which celebrates the boats that carry cars and people across some of the smaller rivers in our area, is called "I believe in ferries." Eric likes depicting places here on Delmarva that are not typically covered by other artists. His prints evoke the laid-back lifestyle people love about our region with an optimistic quality and a sense of humor.

Woodworker Mike Quattrociocchi has also reached a master's status through a lifetime of practice and great attention to detail. He began making things in the family woodshop as a kid and always kept his hand in it even during his career in computer based training at GE and Lockheed Martin. When he retired to Milford, Delaware, he began working with wood full time. His elegant boxes and cabinets are inspired by the Mission style of design. Their perfect simplicity belies the master craftsman's skill with which they are constructed. Mike says he is always trying to push his work "past the functional into a real fine art piece". Indeed, he succeeds with exquisite pieces that allow the natural beauty of the wood and pristine workmanship to sing together in harmony.

Jason Giusti, a glass artist from Showell, Maryland, also has a design sensibility based on simple elegant lines. His love of making art combined with the

Erick Sahler

ericksahler.com

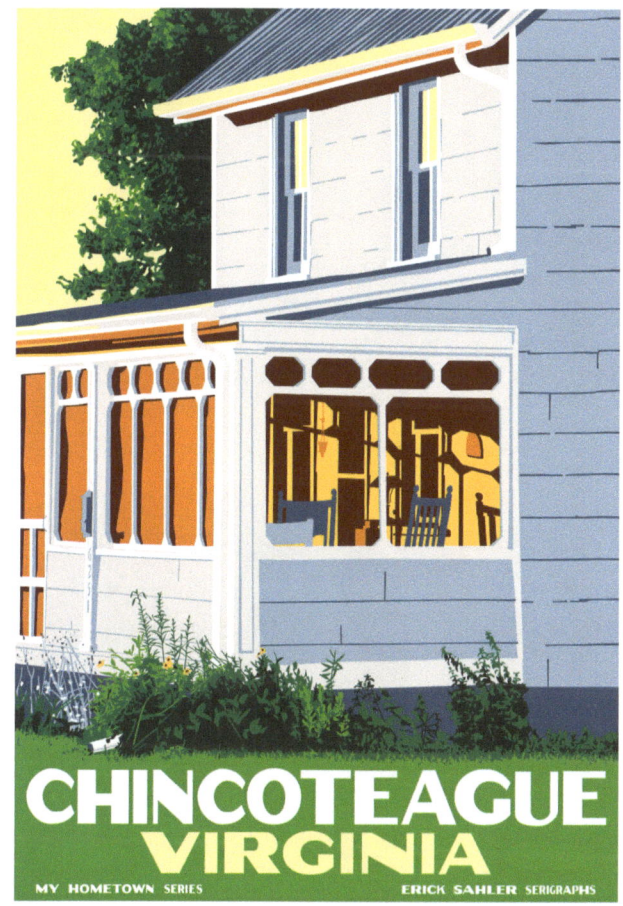

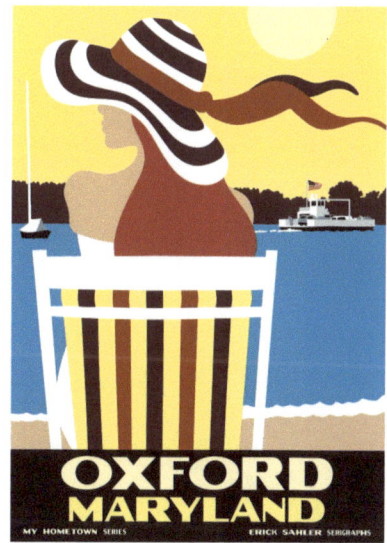

The Strand
(2017) Silkscreen Print

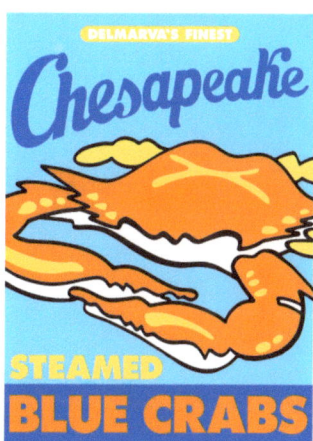

Summer Sunset
(2015) Silkscreen Print

Blue Crabs
(2013) Silkscreen Print

Mike Quattrociocchi

quattrociocchiwoodwork.com

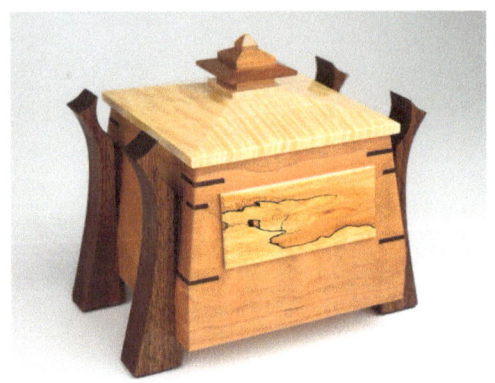

Treasure Box
(2016) Carved and Inlaid Woods

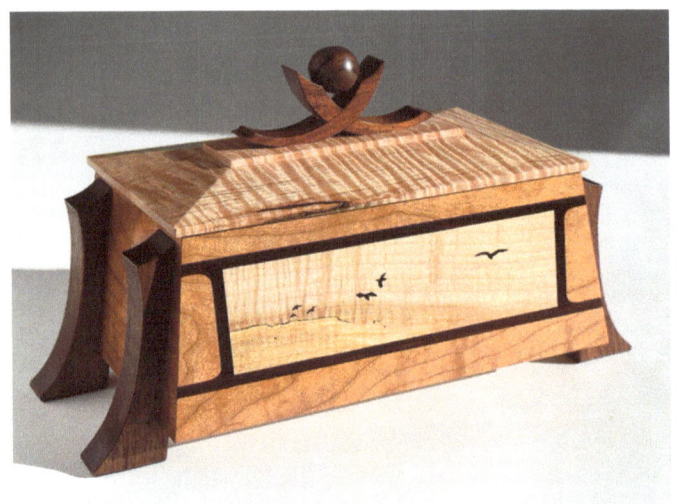

Flight - Series 2
(2016) Carved and Inlaid Woods

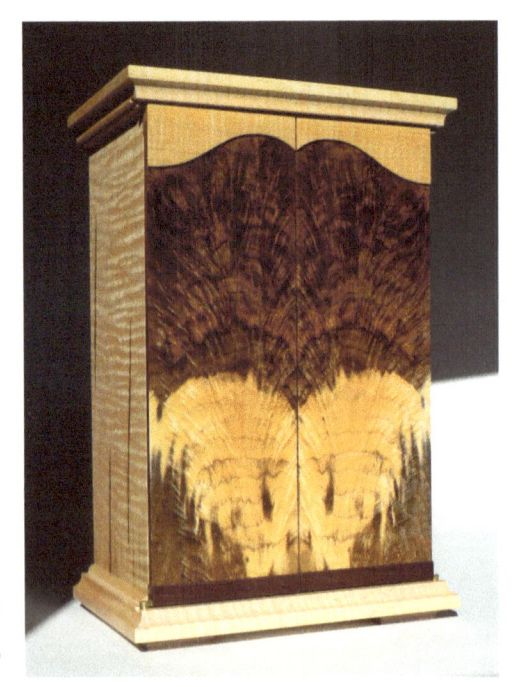

Fan Dancer 2
(2017) Carved and Inlaid Woods

enjoyment of sitting around a campfire with friends and family made the fiery process of blowing glass a natural fit for him as an artist. Jason's most important tool and his muse are one and the same: the fire. Glassmaking techniques have been around since ancient times. The first rule of learning this medium is: safety first. A lack of discipline can result in serious injury. Setting up takes three times as long as actually executing a piece. Jason's work is an alchemy between his knowledge, skill, and a sometimes-unpredictable collaborator: the fire.

Fiber artist Monika Lilley was raised by creative parents on a working farm outside of Berlin, Maryland. The daily discipline of helping with younger siblings and caring for animals, especially the sheep, gave her the foundation she needed to create and teach her art. There are myriad ways to create with fibers. Monika concentrates on weaving and felting. Both of these are time honored techniques which can be as simple or as complex as an artist wants to make them. Monika uses felt work to create paintings rather than functional cloth. They are created with unspun fibers that are matted and interlocked with barbed needles. Her end results are images of landscapes which invoke the wonder of nature.

Ocean City artist Betsy Hall Harrison is also both a fiber artist and a painter, creating her work using another ancient technique: batik. Working primarily on silk, Betsy begins painting light colors then applies hot wax to mask those areas she wants to remain light. When this has cooled it is cracked exposing a web-like network of lines which are painted with darker colors. This process is repeated until Betsy is satisfied with what she has done and then all the wax is removed to reveal the finished painting with its seemingly random marbleized appearance. Betsey's scenes of life near the ocean have a spontaneous moody attitude which bely the careful process of their development.

This is also true of the work of Berlin painter Kirk McBride who began his creative career as a graphic designer in commercial retail print media. When he first started,

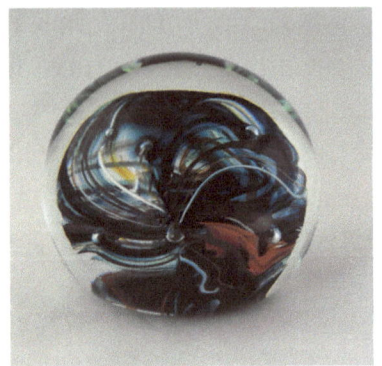

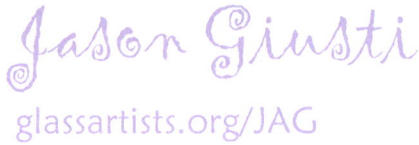

Nebula
(2016) Glass Paperweight

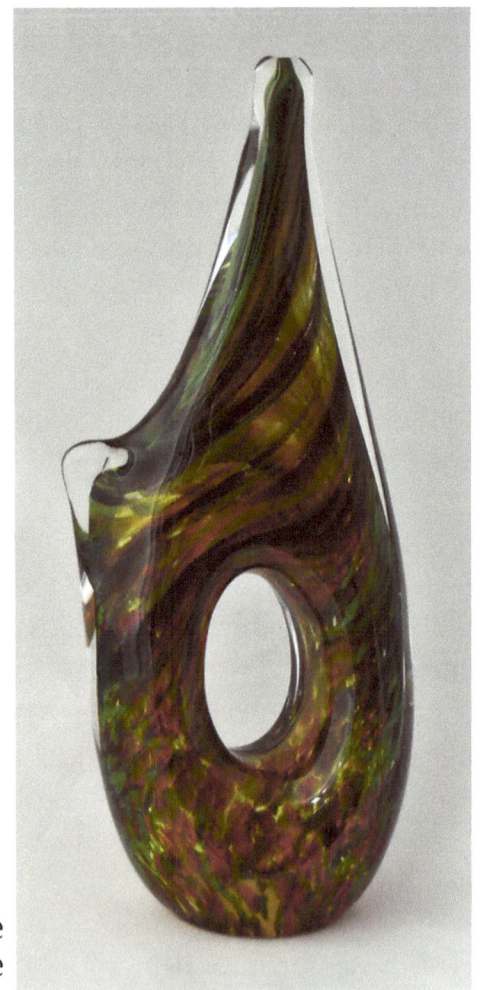

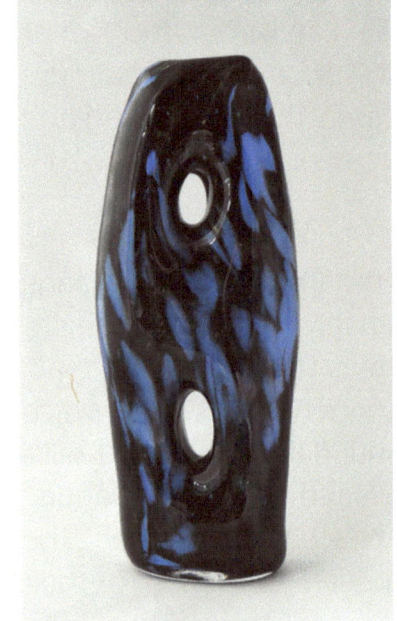

Emergence
(2016) Glass Sculpture

Pinnacle
(2016) Glass Sculpture

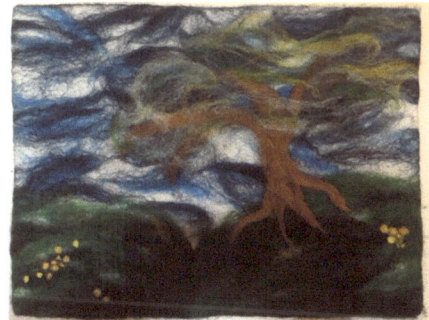

Like A Mighty Oak
(2012) Felted Fiber

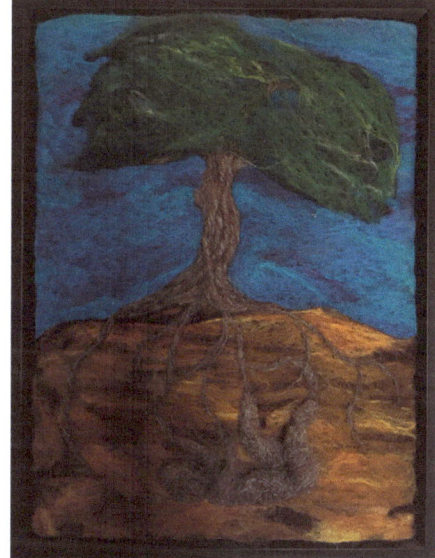

Monika Lilley
facebook.com/monika.lilley

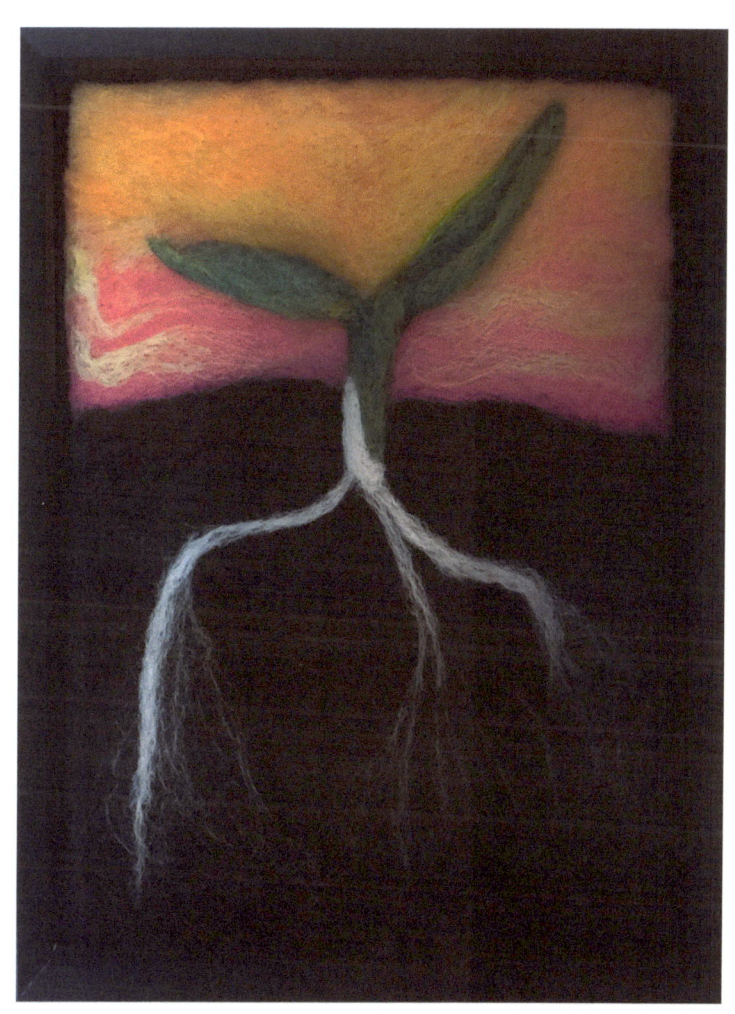

Dust To Dust
(2012) Felted Fiber

In The Beginning...
(2014) Felted Fiber

Betsy Hall Harrison

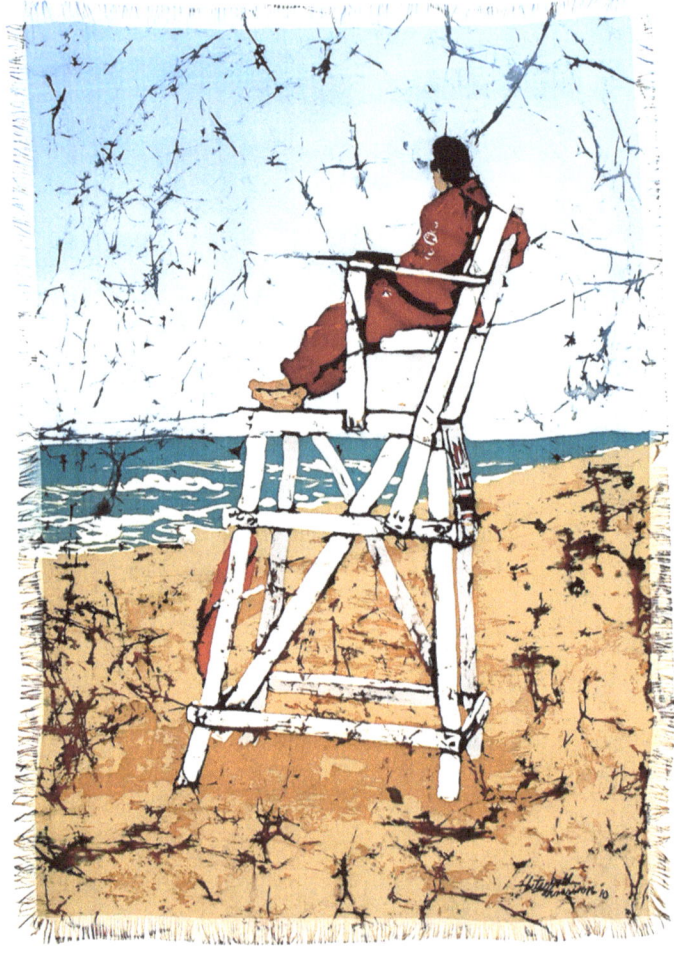

Lifeguard
(2010) Batik on Silk

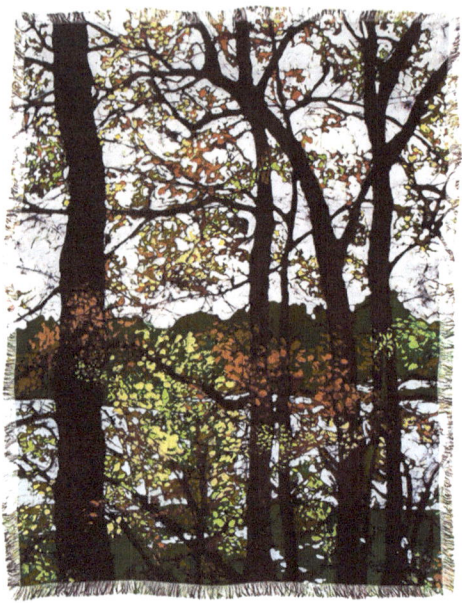

Woodside
(2009) Batik on Silk

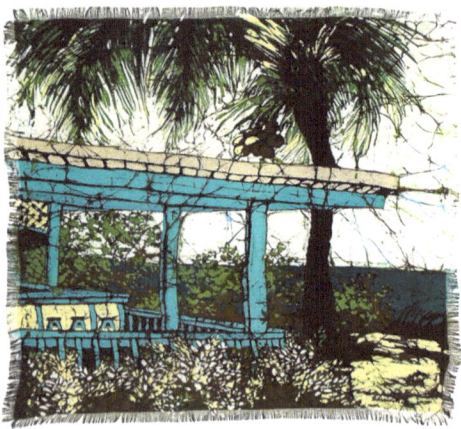

Corner Bar
(2009) Batik on Silk

this sort of work required fastidious work habits which were necessary to create professional printable graphic art. That became ingrained in Kirk who keeps one of the tidiest works spaces of any artist I know. You'd think that mindset would lead to rigid lifeless imagery. Quite the contrary. Kirk's approach may be deliberate and thoughtful, but he paints in an expressive Impressionist style with brush strokes that flow with an easy casual grace. He paints scenes close to home and around the world. Kirk's paintings are inspired by those special moments when the light plays across the landscape - making magic.

Another painter who makes the difficult look easy is Lois Engberg of Salisbury, Maryland. She has found a way to bring together several things she loves: painting, antiques, and gardening. She creates classic oils with elements of each of these things. Lois has been greatly influenced by masters such as Henri Fantin-Latour. Dramatic light and shadow capture the delicate beauty of her flowers and other charming treasures. Lois takes a very exacting style and paints works which evoke a sense of both formal realism and easy optimism.

Snow Hill painter Fred Sprock says his creative discipline comes from a joyful place. "I like painting. So, I could paint seven days a week. So, for me it is easy. I don't wait on the muse. Some days you don't get anything done. But if I were a banker, if the muse did not strike, I don't get to not go to the bank or the insurance company, or whatever. So, you kind of have to be in the studio or outside. But for me it's rarely a chore. It's always a pleasure. So, that's the work ethic. There is no work ethic. It's a fun ethic."

The one artist who typifies this phenomenon of making a flawless work of art look as if it was done with very little effort is Lillian Rippa of Smyrna, Delaware. This chapter is really dedicated to her. At the time of our interview she was 84 and she

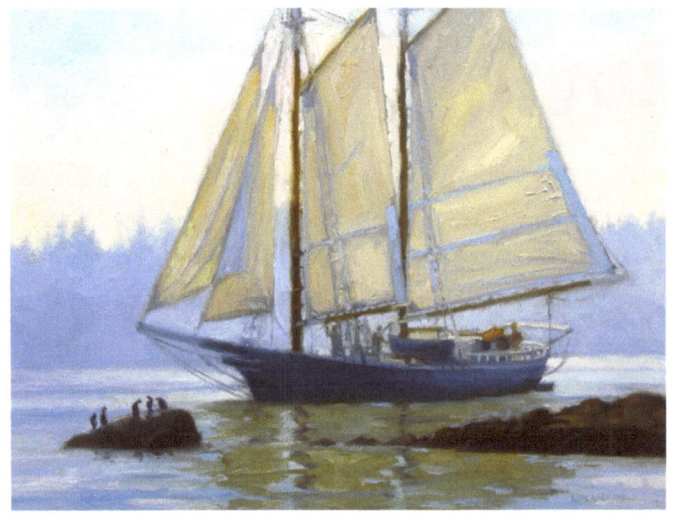

Twisted Sycamore
(2013) Oil

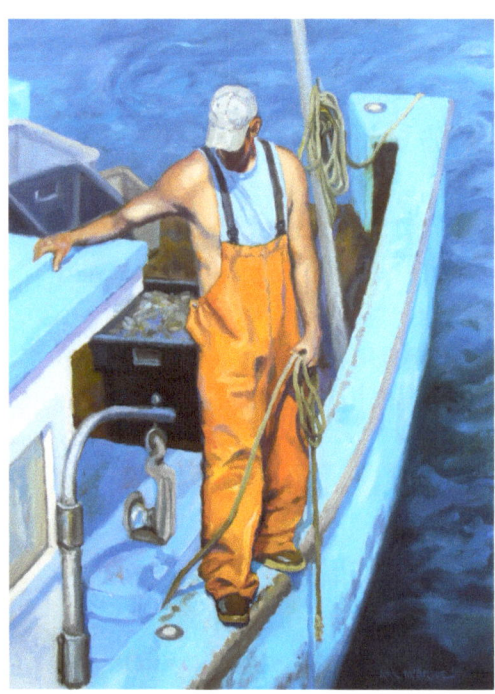

Coming Into The Dock
(2015) Oil

Cormorant's Welcome
(2016) Oil

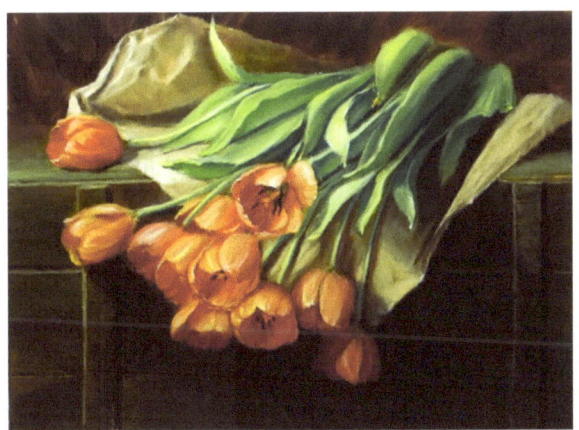

Lois Engberg
loisengberg.com

Market Tulips
(2017) Oil on canvas

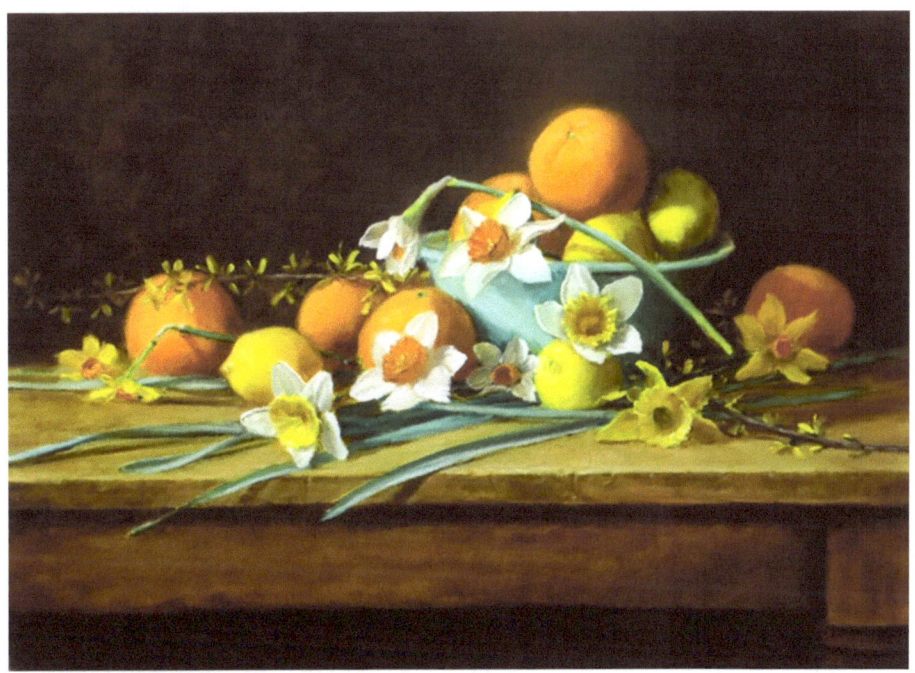

Spring Serenade
(2017) Oil on canvas

Fred Sprock

fredsprock.com

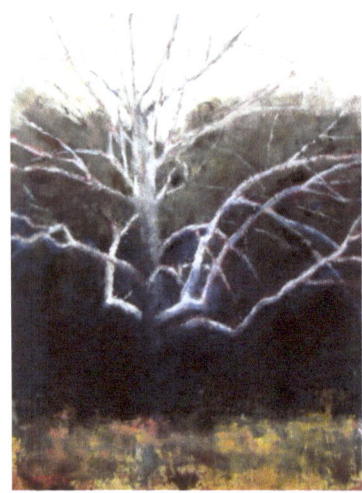

Sycamore Study
(2017) Oils

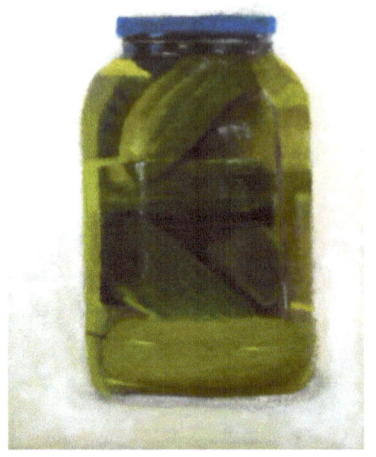

Dill Life With Jar
(2017) Oils

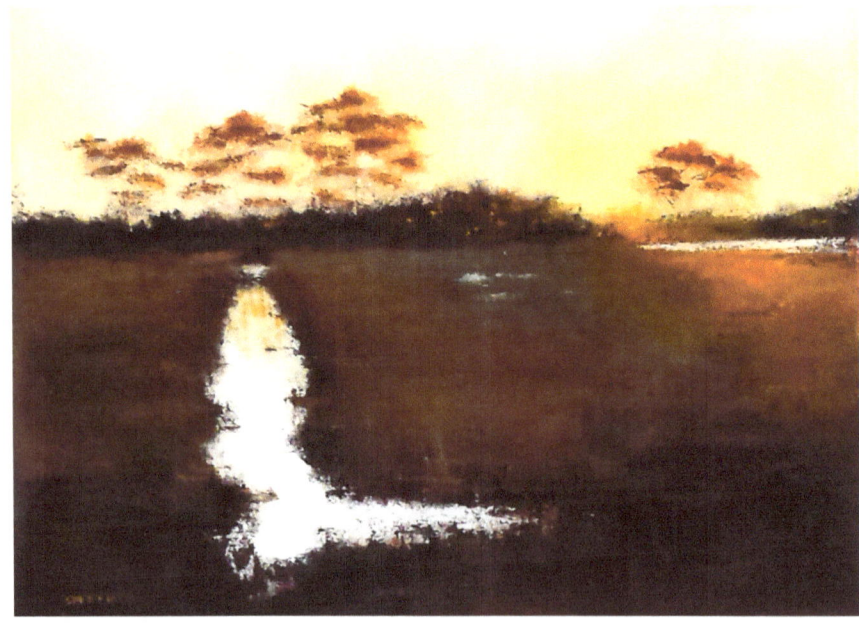

Taps
(2017) Oils

had amazing energy. Lillian practices her brushstrokes just about every day. She said years of teaching in a Montessori school inspired her work philosophy: "There is no freedom without discipline."

When Lillian took up Chinese brush painting she studied under a master named Professor I-Hsiung Ju. He taught the classic ancient traditions of free-style Chinese painting. This begins with practicing the brush strokes that create what are known as the four gentlemen: the chrysanthemum, the orchid, the bamboo, and the plum. These four plants contain all the basic strokes needed to paint just about anything else. Lillian says that she worked over a year on just the bamboo or bone stroke which is used frequently in calligraphy.

Lillian had this to say about her training and now daily discipline: "There's no pencil on the paper and you have to know your subject. You have to know the strokes you want to use before you start your painting. Then you have the freedom to do whatever you want. But you have to master that. So, if I put a stroke down on the paper, and I am not strong or I am weak, or I am not interested, it shows. And, it looks shaky."

Art forms, like Chinese brush painting, have a reverence for everything thing from the process to the materials themselves. In some ways Lillian's painting is a collaboration with other artisans. The ink, the grinding stone, the brush, and the paper, which are called the four treasures; are all handmade. Even their containers have all been carefully produced using ancient traditions handed down through families. They are beautiful in and of themselves. And so are Lillian's paintings.

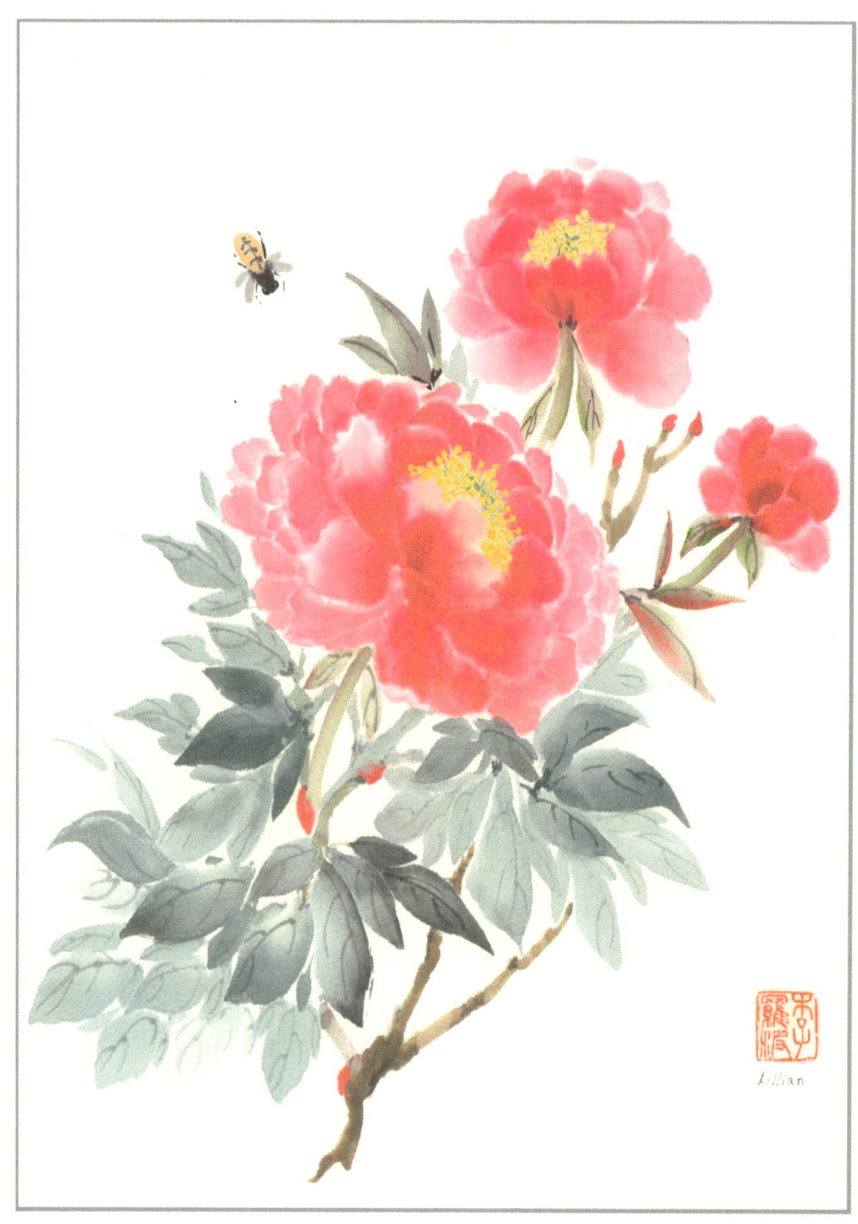

A Pollen Sighting
(2010) Chinese ink
and watercolor

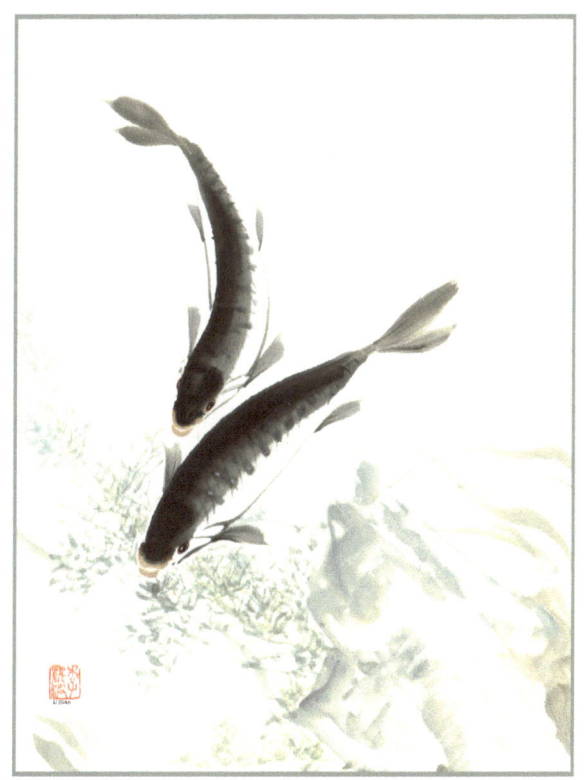

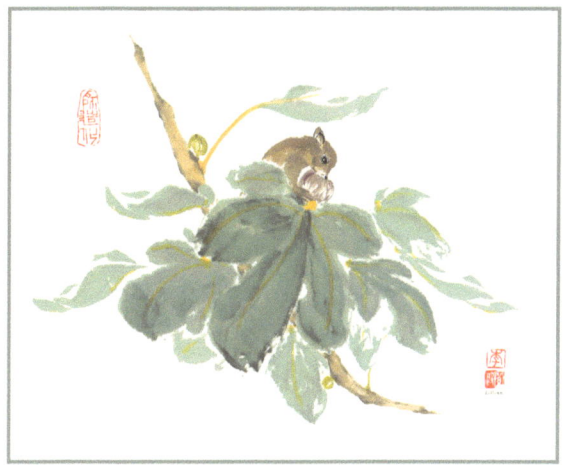

Lillian's Garden - Young Squirrel & Fig I
(2013) Chinese ink and watercolor

Happiness
(2012) Chinese ink and watercolor

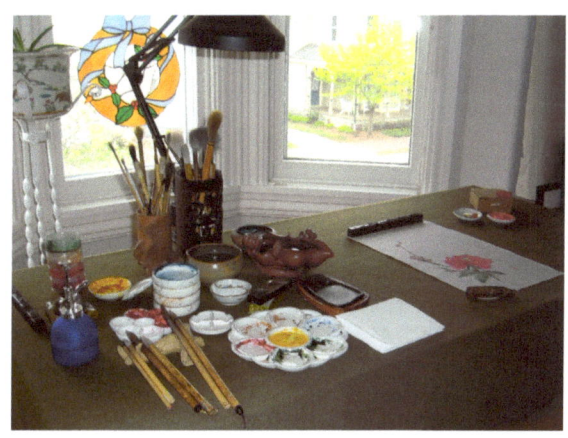

Painting Table Layout
(2017) Digital Photograph

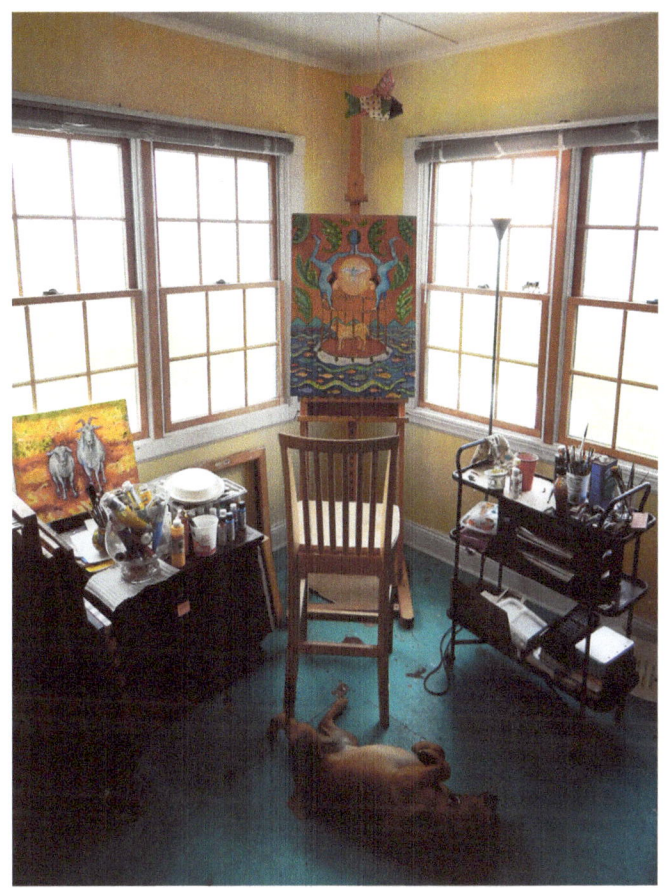

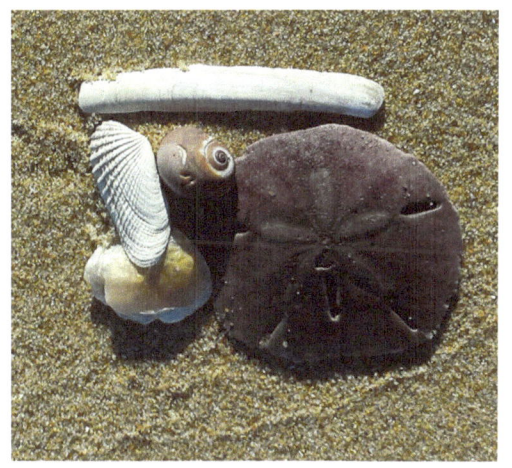

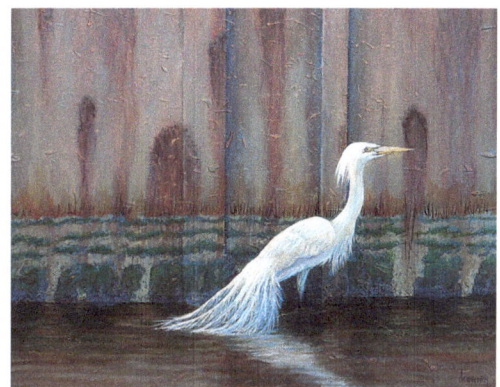

The Land of Pleasant Living

Visitors come to Delmarva for beach vacations and decide to stay year-round because they find a pace of life that is less hectic than the one they left. Folks who are born and raised here stay because they too appreciate the laidback lifestyle. Certainly, artists settle here for that reason too, but they have other reasons. One reason is purely practical. The Delmarva peninsula is conveniently located within a day's drive of New York, Philadelphia, Baltimore, and Washington D.C. all which provide opportunities to see and sell art. More importantly, artists value the clarity and intensity of the light created by a mostly flat landmass surrounded by great bodies of reflective water. Finally, there is an abundance of inspiration in the scenery and wildlife of this region.

Jim Adcock is an accomplished painter, cartoonist, and caricature artist. He is most well-known for his paintings of local towns and life at the beach. Jim works both from life and his own photographs. His work is a celebration of all that he sees, particularly that which can be found right here in Worcester County, Maryland. Jim finds unlimited subject matter in the local scenery of this place he calls home. His approach is to look around and appreciate the charm of everyday ordinary things and places. Jim says, "There is beauty everywhere, but particularly on the Eastern Shore."

Salisbury painter Myrna McGrath also celebrates the region with her work. Myrna began her career in art owning a framing shop. She became a well-known and widely collected Eastern Shore artist with her prints of her hand drawn maps illustrated thematically with lighthouses, ducks, crabs, or other familiar symbols of Delmarva. Landscapes, flowers, and birds populate Myrna's paintings. For her making art is a matter of balancing practical goals with inspiration and sometimes whimsy. She says that the best advice she ever got about making art was to "relax and let the paint paint."

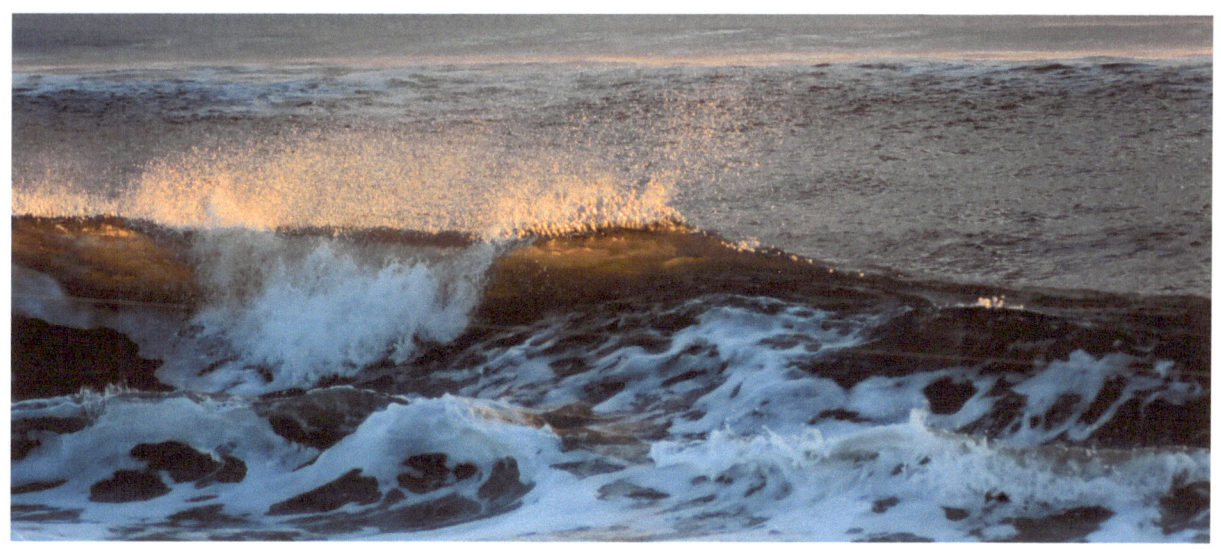

Dana Kester-McCabe
Assateague Sunrise
(2017) Digital Photograph

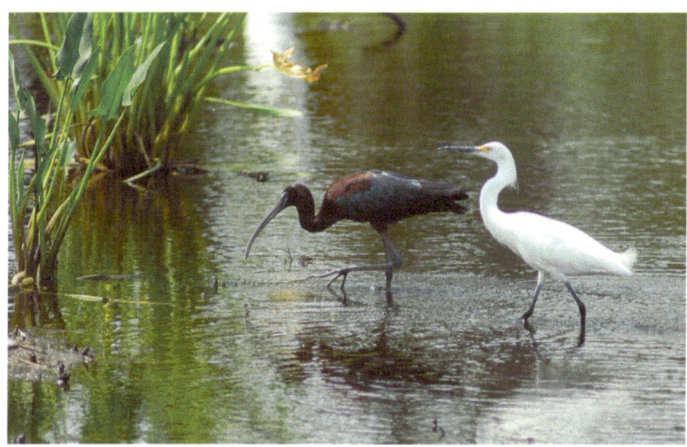

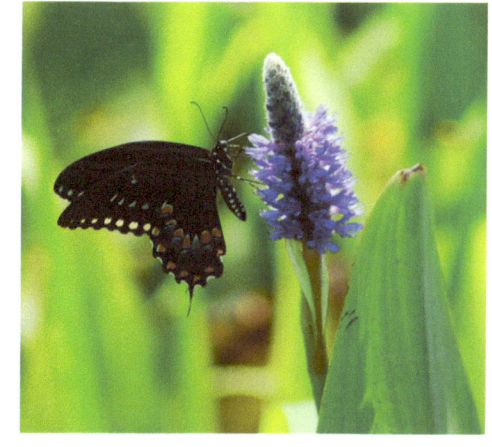

Dana Kester-McCabe
Ibis and Egret
(2009) Digital Photograph

Dana Kester-McCabe
Black Swallow Tail
(2016) Digital Photograph

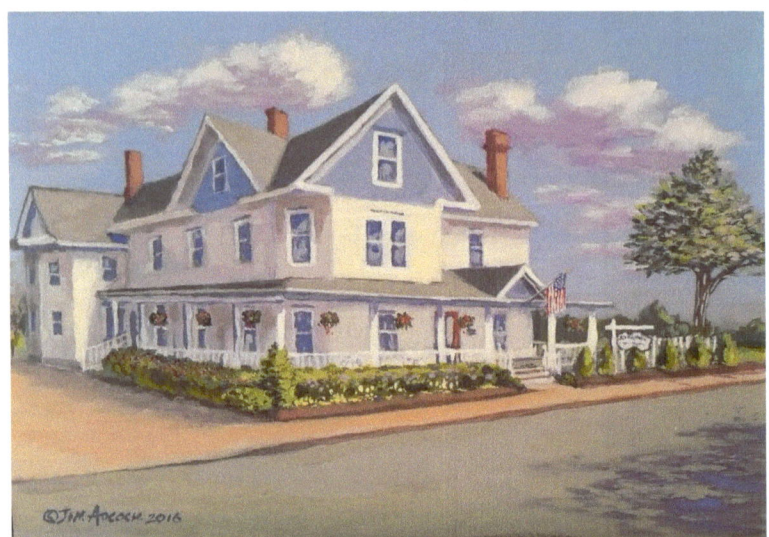

Miss Molly's Inn
(2016) Acrylic

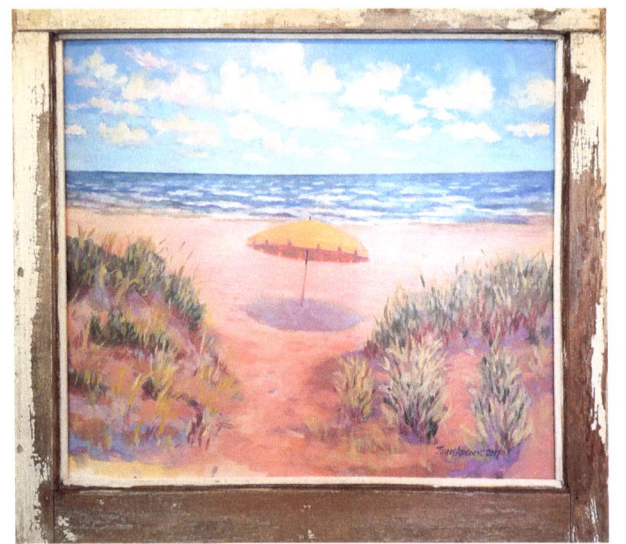

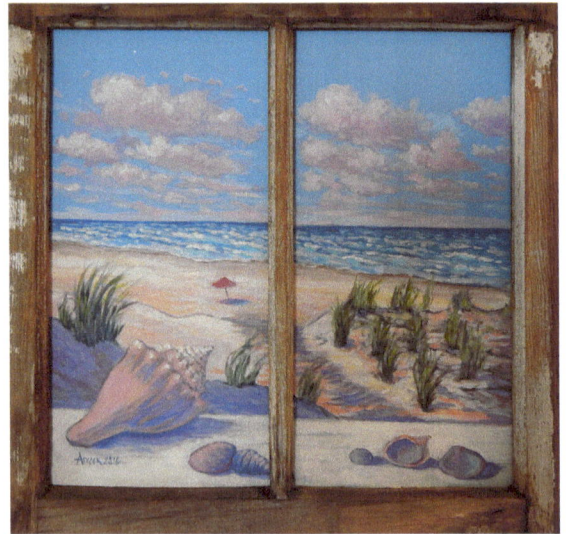

Yellow Beach Umbrella
(2017) Acrylic

Red Beach Umbrella
(2015) Acrylic

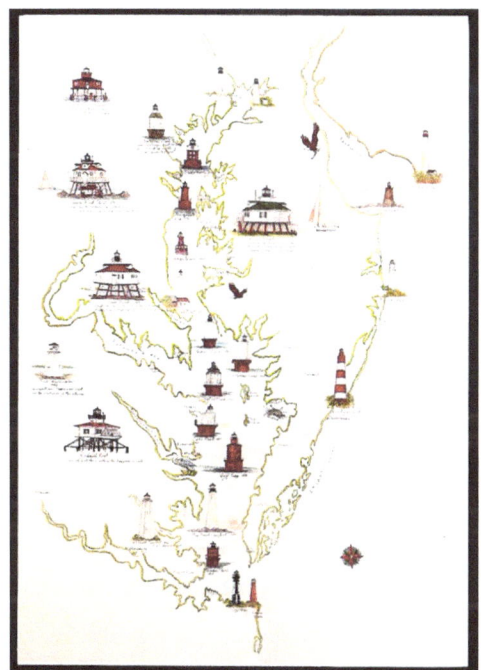

A Little Marsh Magic
Print of watercolor painting

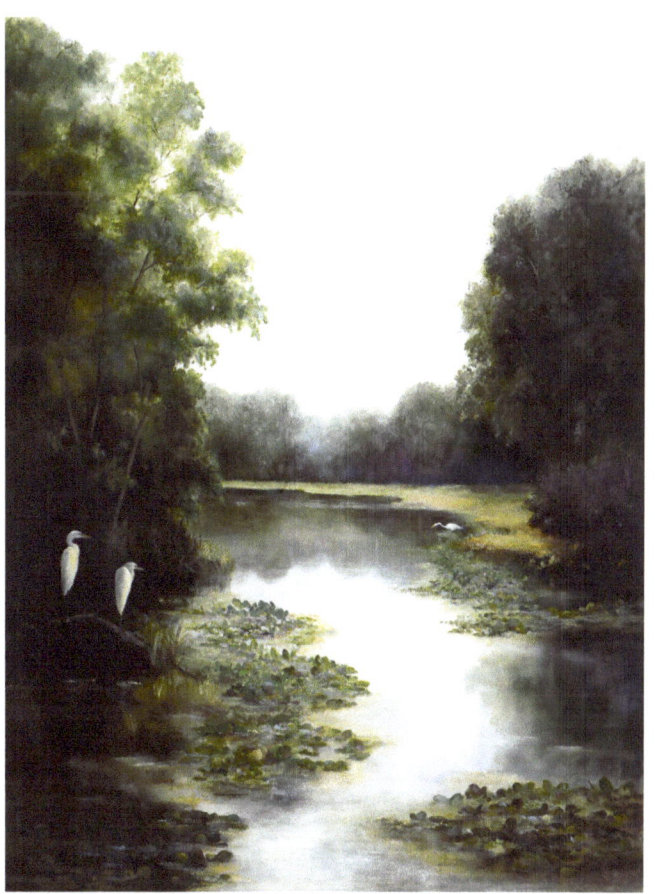

Mears Creek
Print of oil painting

Lighthouses of the Chesapeake Bay
Print of watercolor painting

Celebrating a sense of place is a common theme of Delmarva artists. An artist with a graphic approach to this is Rafael Reyes, of Ocean Pines Maryland, who creates paintings and inlaid wood bas reliefs. His works combine multiple images in a stylized kaleidoscopic effect. This abstraction and layering give the viewer an intriguing visual puzzle to sort out. Rafael's works combining the Maryland flag with the American flag or sports mascots are very popular for their joyful regional pride.

Susan Mayberry is a Queenstown artist who works with an eclectic set of mediums, such as the dried and cleaned shells of steamed blue crabs which she seals and paints to create lovely Christmas ornaments. Susan makes her living as a muralist and faux finisher as well as through her painting commissions. She says she has a sort of inner dance between the practical and the creative: "I do approach things from an intellectual perspective, and then I try to not let it interfere too much with the process and let my emotions or the spiritual ideas flow, or take over."

Bishopville artist John Iamperi carries on a tradition that began in certain neighborhoods of Baltimore, across the bay, where front door screens are painted with landscapes, wildlife, and other charming subjects. The paintings provide privacy from street-side passers-by who cannot see in, while allowing in air and an undisrupted view from inside the house. These painted screens add color and joy to the lives of John's patrons. They also reflect the deep cultural connection on Delmarva provided by all the people who have moved here from the Baltimore-Washington D.C. area.

Lesley McCaskill is one such émigré. She moved to lower Delaware, after a long career as an art teacher in Bethesda Maryland. Lesley works primarily in watercolors. Her paintings are optimistic with a bright cheery color palette. These reflect her personality and her love for her surroundings. "Being a gardener, and being someone who really appreciates nature, I find it is where I am happiest, and where I learn so much. It gives me an emotional connection to the scenery." Leslie

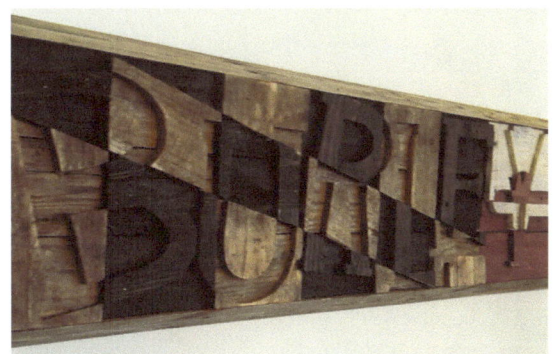

Burley Sign
(2016) Carved
Painted Wood

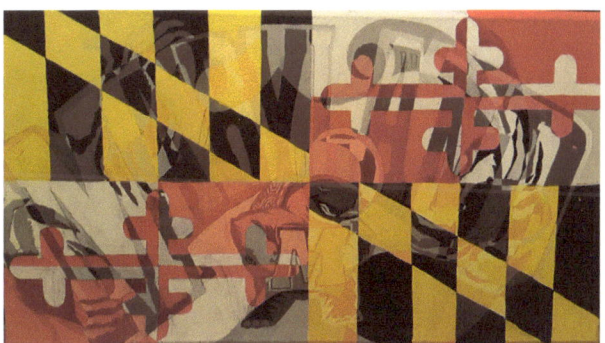

Maryland Flag - Terp
Abstraction
(2016) Acrylic

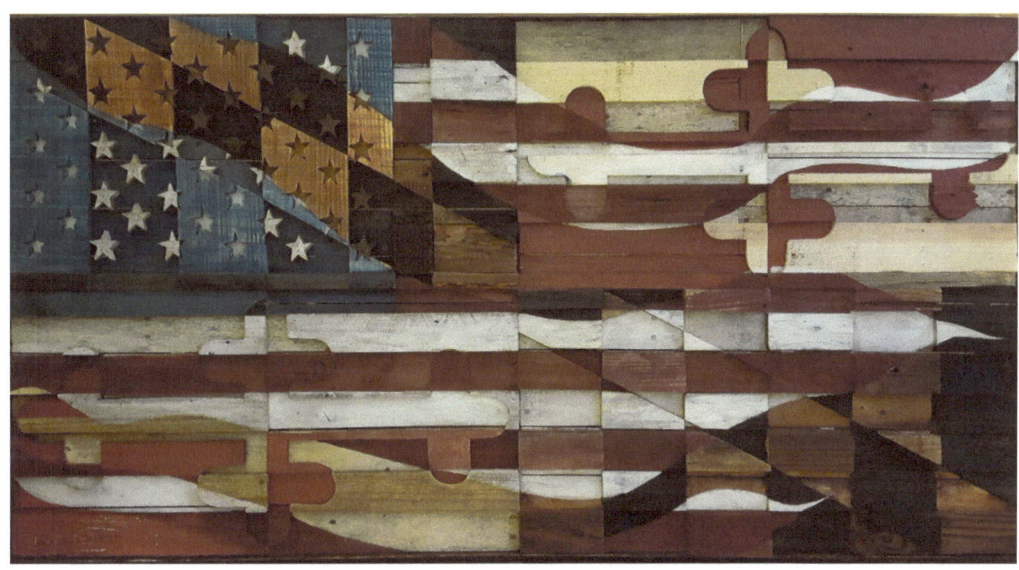

American and Maryland Flags
(2016) Carved Painted Wood

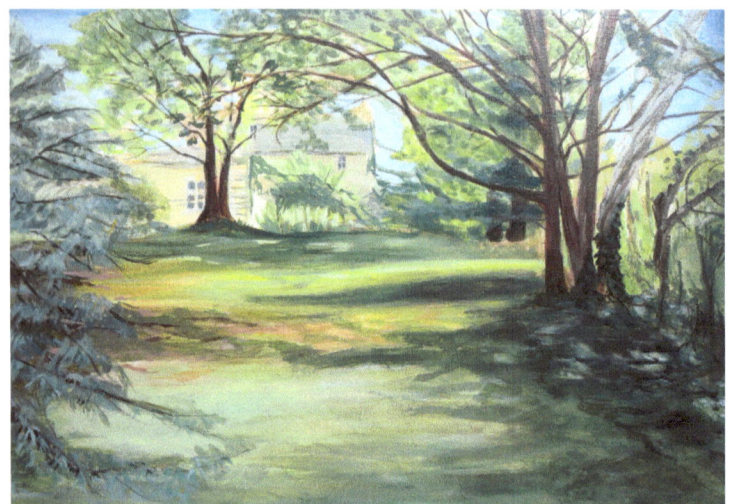

susanmayberry.com

Miss Kitty's Haven
(2006) Oils

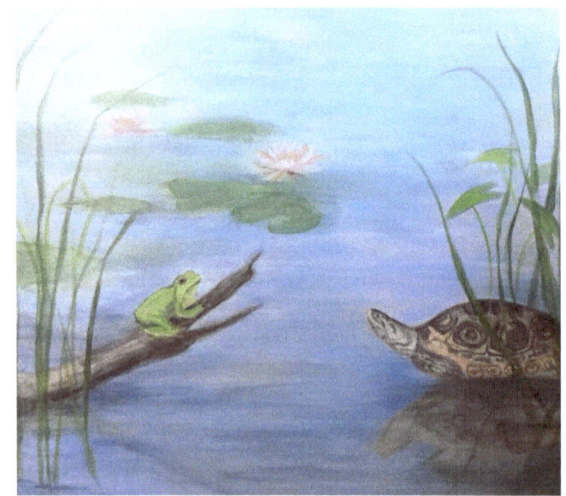

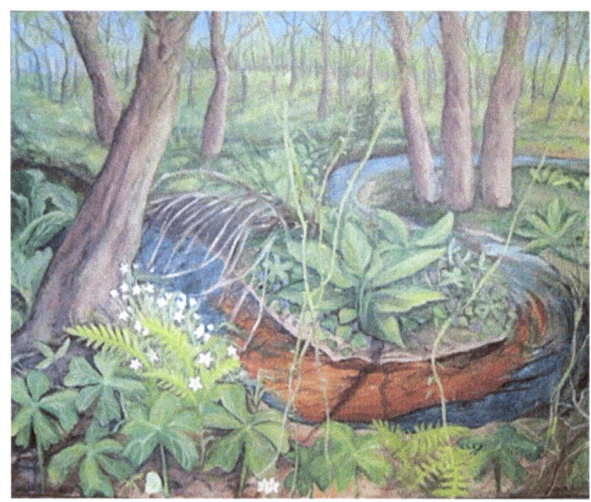

Pond Meeting
(2016) Acrylic Mural on Wallboard

Spring Beauty
(2002) Oils

John Iampieri

paintedscreensonline.com

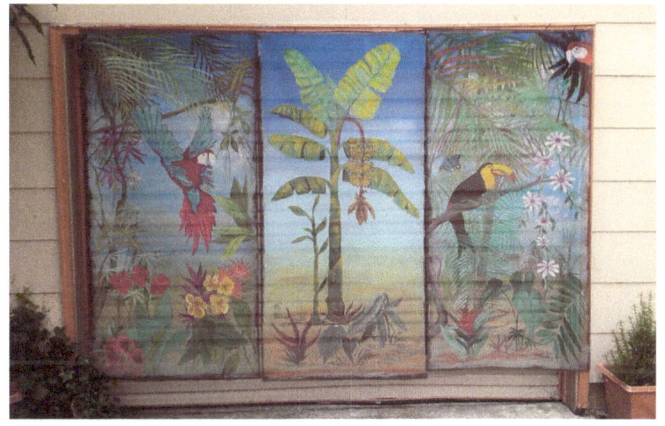

Hawaii Bound
(2016) Vinyl Door Screens

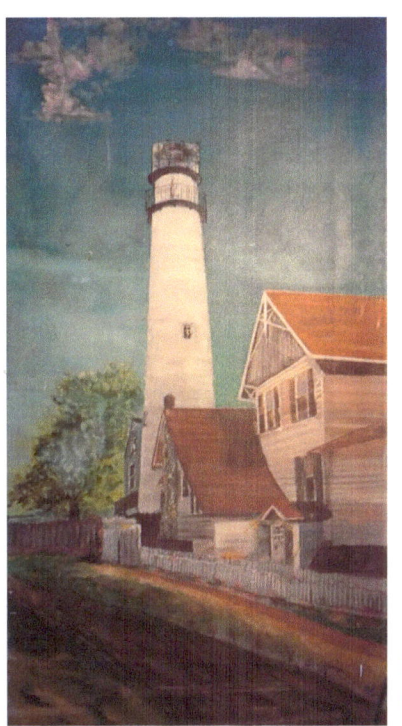

White Marlins Out To Water
(2016) Vinyl Door Screens

Fenwick Island Lighthouse
(2016) Vinyl Door Screens

Wizard of Oz Smokehouse
(2016) Watercolor

Lesley McCaskill
facebook.com/lesley.mccaskill

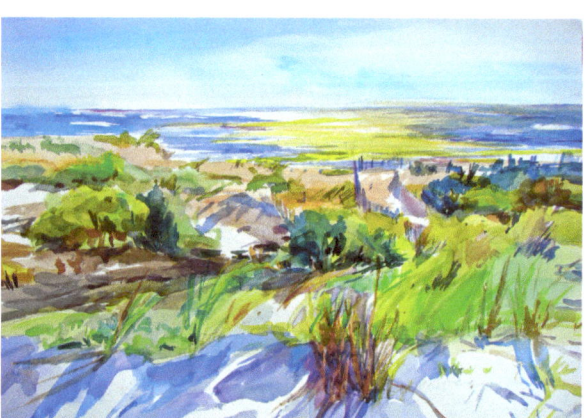

Spring Rain
(2016) Watercolor

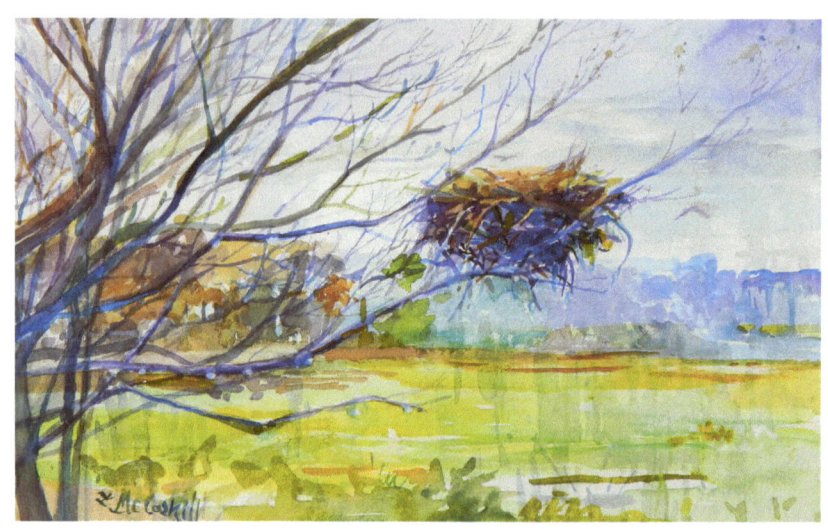

Sunrise at Cape Henlopen
(2016) Watercolor

begins each painting with quick "thumbnail" sketches to which she assigns a word or phrase describing the feeling of a scene. She begins many of her paintings outside on site. These sketches and their associated words help reconnect her to the initial experience when she puts finishing touches on the work back in the studio.

Pastel painter Nick Serratore grew up outside of Philadelphia. He first became known to the Delmarva arts community working as a gallery manager for the venerable Rehoboth Art League. Now he paints full time and is a founding member of the Milton Arts Guild and the Studios on Walnut, in Milton, Delaware. In addition to the usual landscapes and seascapes that one might expect for our region, Nick finds great inspiration in the wild meadows and woodlands here, which allow him to explore the full range of colors and textures that lend themselves so well to his chosen medium of pastels. In those works, he brings to life some of the magical places of the region which tourists sometimes miss.

Watercolor painter Nancy Mysak grew up on the Eastern Shore and continues to live and paint in Eden, Maryland. Like many watercolorists Nancy treats each piece as an experiment combining mercurial transparent washes with controlled detailed brushwork. Nancy's subject matter celebrates life on the water here. Her paintings are light and airy. When preparing for the task of taking her work to a show, facing potential criticism and the uncertainty of sales, Nancy wraps her art work in quilts made by women in her family. For Nancy these blankets, which were passed down to her from her mother and her grandmothers, symbolize the unconditional support they gave for her work. Nancy's paintings connect the beauty all around her in the present to the deep spiritual roots of this place and her family's love.

The people and traditions of this region provide rich sources for creative expression. At the same time this place, which is often referred to as the "land of pleasant living", is itself a compelling subject. Authors often make a place in their

Nick Serratore

serratoreart.com

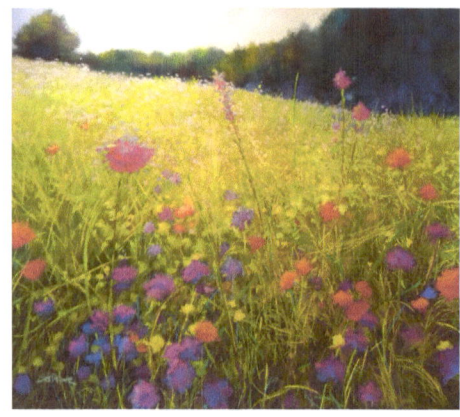

Wild Things
(2017) Pastel

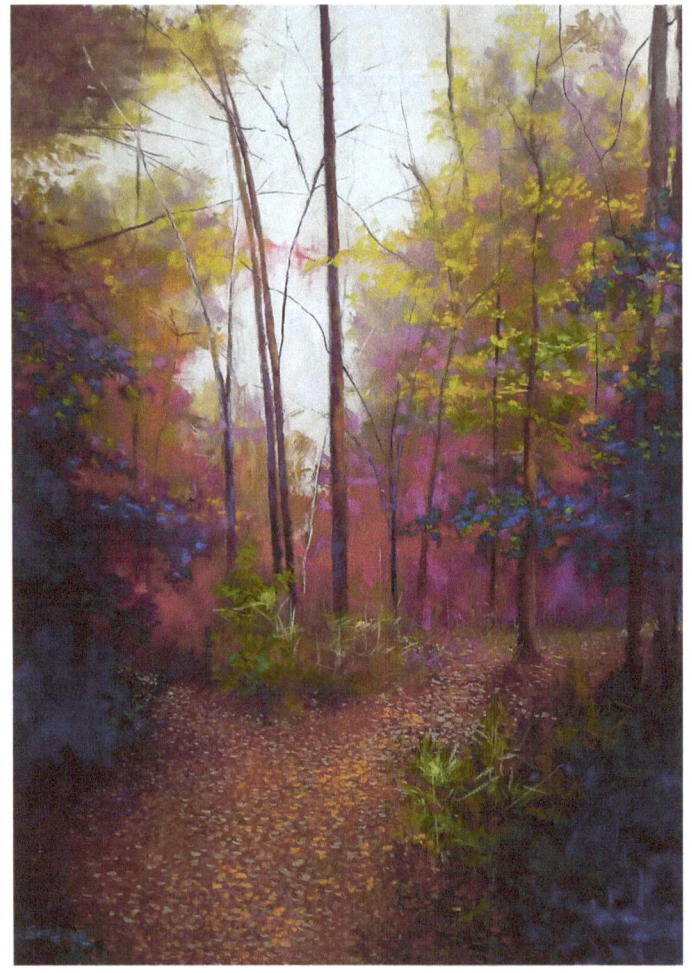

Prime Hook Trail
(2016) Pastel

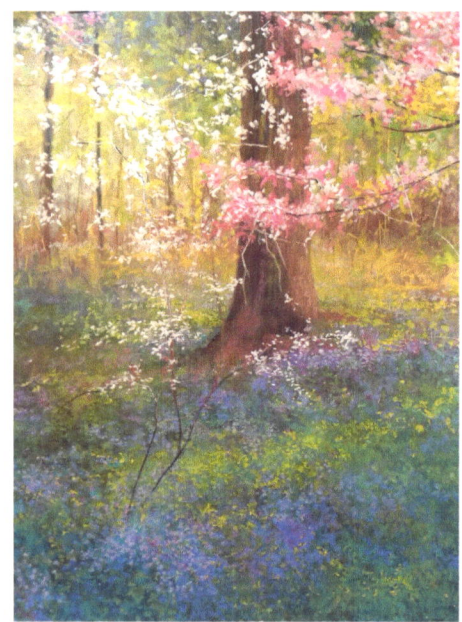

The Rite of Spring
(2017) Pastel

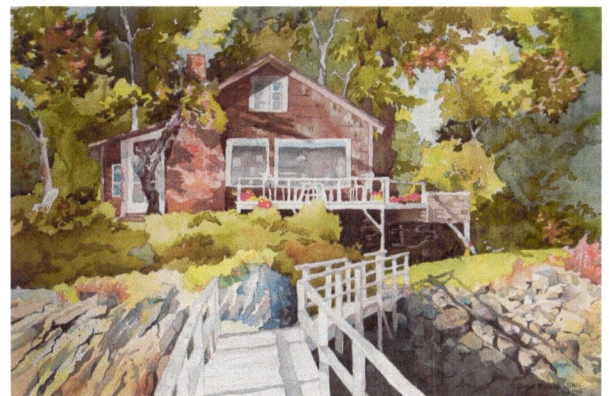

Piney Point
(2016) Watercolor

Old Ship's Lines
(2017) Watercolor

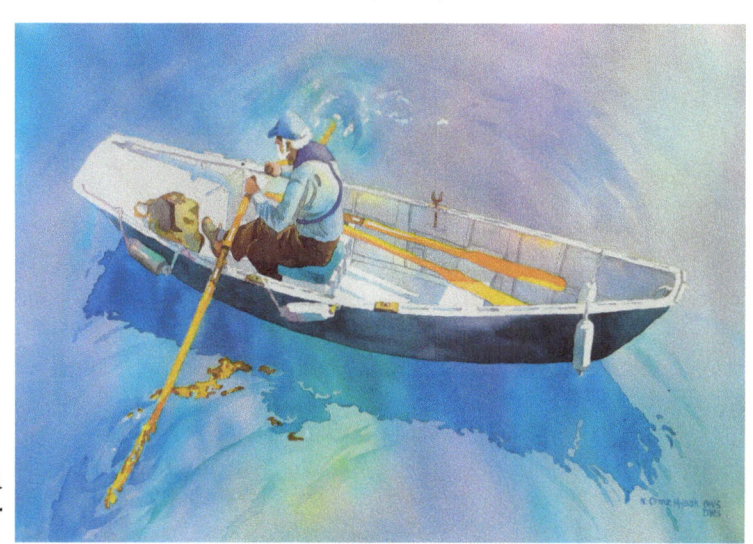

Old Man and the Sea
(2016) Watercolor

stories serve as a character. Its unique aspects have that much impact on the people they write about. Visual artists likewise see their surroundings as more than mere inspiration. They have a relationship with the place they work in.

Milton artist Denise Dumont moved to the Delmarva coast in part because it reminded her of Long Island, New York, where she was raised. There is no mistaking a Denise Dumont painting. It is without a doubt Impressionistic. Her brush work appears quick and gestural. At the same time, it shows a practiced hand that accurately captures the essence of a scene. Her pastoral compositions are built with subtle serene hues. She says that she is simply responding to what it is she sees or feels in a place. Denise has her favorite scenes to paint. She says they feel like comforting old friends. "I like to paint them in different weather conditions, and just sort of be there. Sometimes what is nice about a spot is just the spot itself apart, you know, from the painting you are going to do. There are a couple of spots where I just like to hear the ocean, or feel the weather, that kind of thing. But I do tend to go back a lot to the same spot. I guess it is a kind of muse in a way."

Whether it is earth, sea, or sky, artists cannot help but respond to the "place characters" who inhabit Delmarva. From the rolling hills of the upper peninsula, to the lush mystery of the forests and swamps, to the big sky country of the flat open marshes, to sunny beaches, or to the majesty and power of the waters beyond our shorelines; they each are like spirits who haunt us. They entice us back again and again, seeming to demand that we record that which is continually changing before our very eyes.

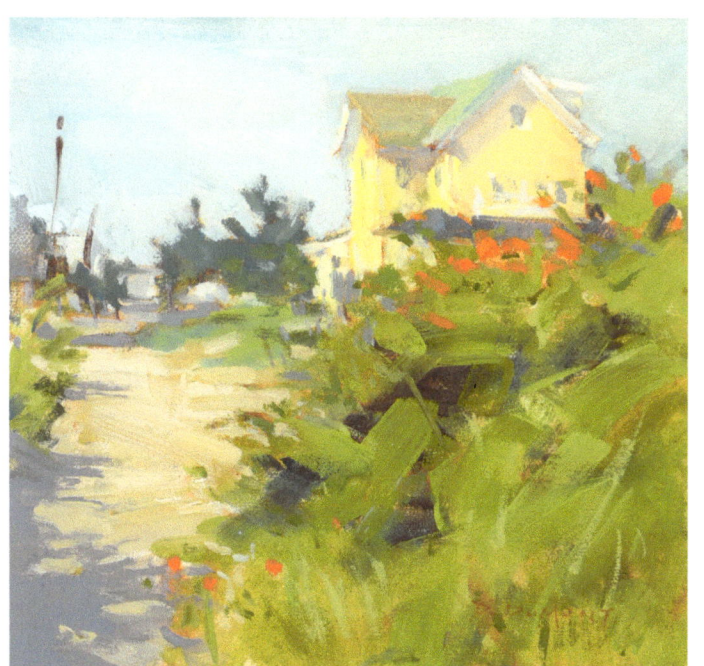

Lewes Beach
(2014) Oil on linen

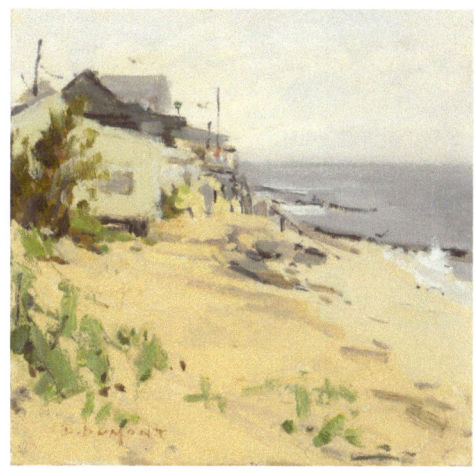

Overcast Afternoon
(2014) Oil on linen

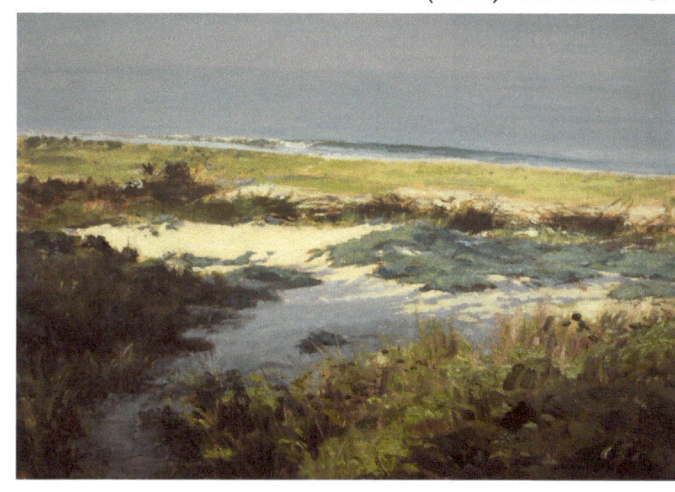

View From The Great Dune
(2014) Oil on linen

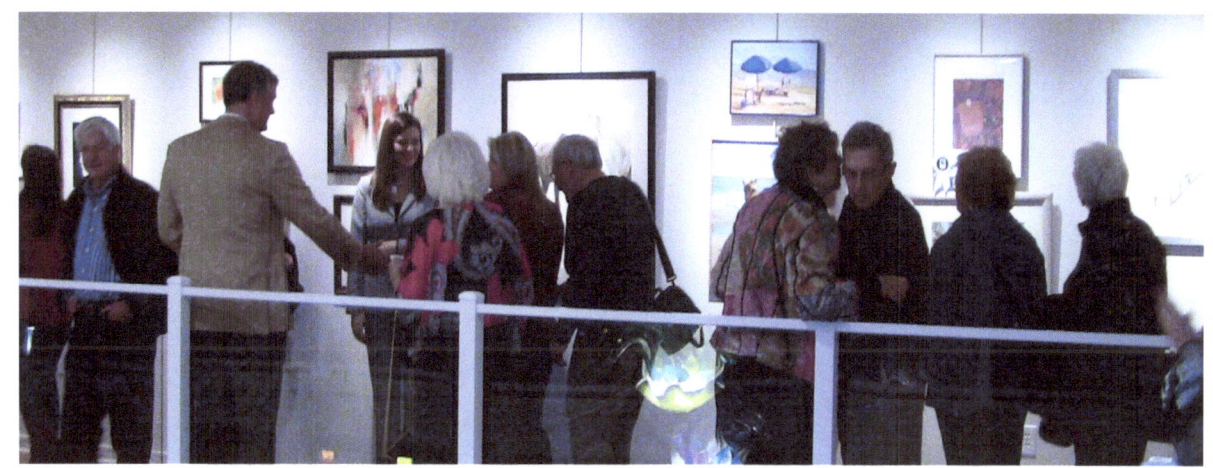

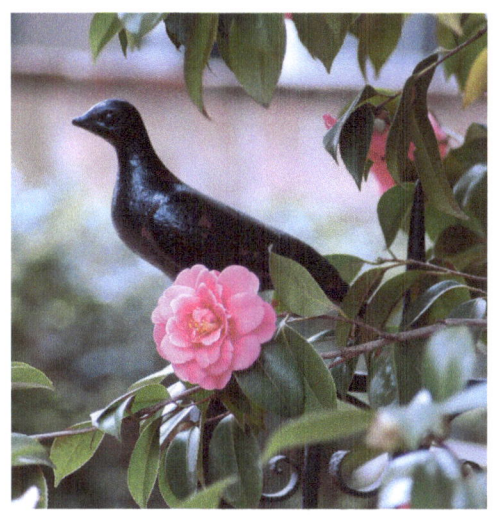

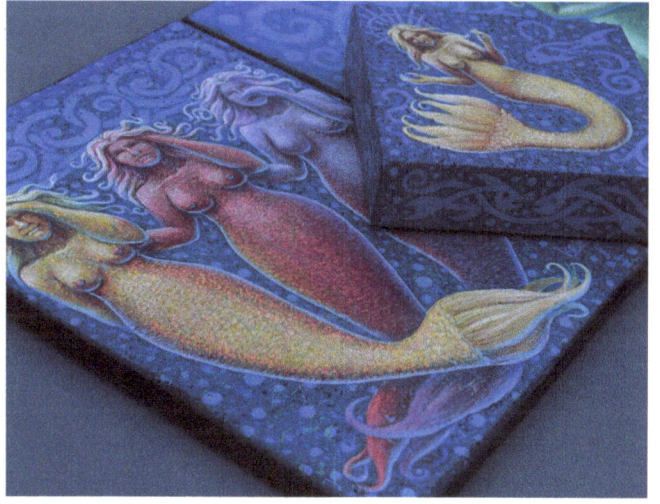

Lessons in Creative Living

Whether you are an artist or just enjoy looking at art, Delmarva has really blossomed in the last few decades. As I mentioned before, there are arts organizations in almost every town with classes and competitive exhibitions for both hobbyists and professionals. Commercial galleries here probably enjoy the same rate of success as galleries anywhere. The good news is that more and more Delmarva galleries are prevailing. We could do better promoting the full diversity of artists here. This is slowly improving and I hope that trend will continue. Meanwhile, the creative variety among artists here on Delmarva never ceases to amaze me. It has been especially wonderful to meet those who have the courage not to just occasionally dabble in new ideas, but to devote every day to them.

Recently the Ocean City Center for the Arts held a show titled "The Divine Feminine Arts Exhibition" which was curated by artists Deb Rolig and Diane Gray. It showed the incredible depth of talent and stylistic range we have here on the shore. There were paintings, sculptures, digital works, video, and a companion book all produced by women about the spiritual aspects of being a woman. The caliber of the show was equal to that of any seen in New York and beyond. This show was not an anomaly. There are shows of this quality throughout the year all around the peninsula.

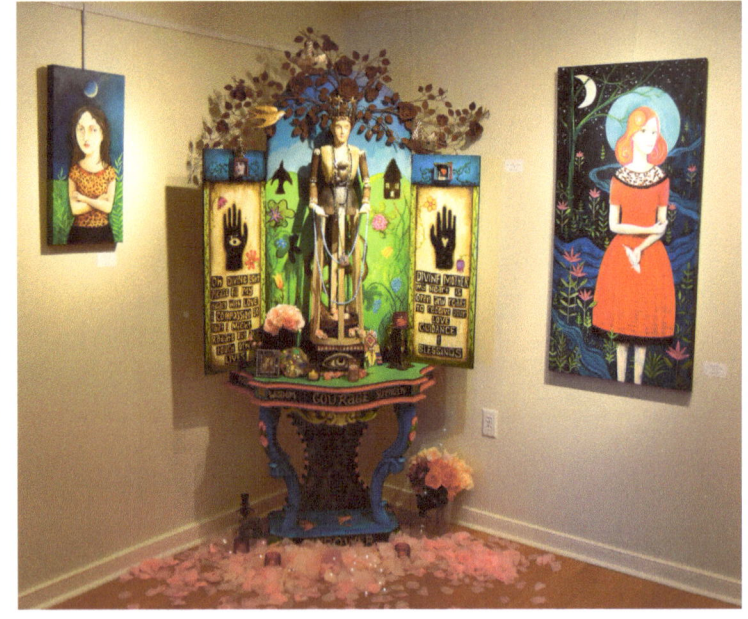

Divine Feminine Show
Ocean City Center for the Arts
(2017) Digital Photograph (Dana Kester-McCabe)

I found all the artists I interviewed uniquely interesting, yet at the same time they generally had a few things in common. First, they all had a sense that they were called to this work. They felt the work was an essential part of who they are. Most had been making art since their early childhood. They may have had artists as relatives who encouraged them, or they may have had to fight to be creative in the face of family disapproval. Either way it was something they simply could not stop doing. Secondly, except for one or two people, the interviewees were all extremely humble people. The stereotype of the egotistical artist did not ring true for these folks. Third, though they all wanted to make a living through their art, they were willing to live with less or maintain a day job to support their artwork. Finally, their approach to life and work could benefit anyone, whether they were an artist or not.

As I bring painting back from my creative background into my daily work again, I am appreciating eight key lessons that I learned anew or for the first time, while talking to these Delmarva artists. They are worth studying for anyone wanting to learn a more creative approach to life.

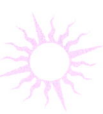

1. Show up every day.

No matter how bad yesterday was - show up ready to work today. No matter how good it may feel resting on yesterday's laurels - show up to work today. When your creative juices run dry practice your technique.

Chinese brush painter, Lillian Rippa talked about how daily practice and intentional preparation helped her to paint each of her paintings with her own soul. My interview with Lillian had special meaning for me because it reminded me of a book my father gave me to read while I was in art school: *The Way of Chinese Painting* by Mai Mai Sze. It described all those brush techniques Lillian spoke of, and it gave insight into how artists capture in paint the essence of their subject matter. Meeting Lillian reminded me that in order to do that you have to show up to the blank paper every day, that "There is no freedom without discipline." No matter what kind of work you do, if every day you bring along your sincere commitment and integrity, you will make progress.

2. Never stop learning.

All the artists I interviewed had an unquenchable curiosity to learn every day from what they were doing or how they might try something new. Some greatly valued getting an education in their chosen field. Some even had advanced degrees. There is, however, no consensus as to whether a college education is necessary to succeed as an artist. Many felt that taking workshops or apprenticing with an established artist allowed for more individual attention and provided valuable professional networking contacts. My suggestion is this: If you love serious scholarship, want the prestige of a degree, or you want to teach college, go for a graduate level education. If you simply want to make a living at your art, take workshops and apply for residencies at artist retreats.

Regardless of what educational path you choose, if you want to make any money at all from your art, be sure that you take some basic business, accounting, and marketing classes. This is the biggest gap found in most post high school level art programs. You can take inexpensive courses in these subjects at any time through your local community college. They will help prepare you for the business of being an artist, which is essentially to be an independent entrepreneur.

Most importantly don't ever let anything discourage you from trying new things that could stretch your knowledge and abilities. An engaged curiosity is the key to a long creative life well lived.

3. Speak up for yourself.

It is essential for artists to learn how to promote their work. There are many reasons artists resist self-promotion. Some people fall in love with making art because they are too shy to communicate well in other ways. Some have to get over the unreasonable fear that their work is simply not good enough. They have developed technical skills to communicate through their chosen medium but not necessarily through press releases, advertising, social media, or -yikes!- public speaking engagements.

Many artists hope they will eventually be able to hire an agent who will take care of these things for them. That doesn't happen until there has been some success, however. In order to have that success, the artist must get the word out about their work. So, all you artists out there who want to quit your day job - or really anyone who wants to - don't be afraid to put yourself out there in the public eye. You will learn a lot and you cannot succeed without doing so.

4. Don't be afraid to learn from failure.
For the artist who is trying to mind their pocket book it is very hard to resist the temptation to get bogged down trying to redeem a project that has failed. No one likes wasting art supplies. Many of the artists I met described long periods of time trying to salvage projects they just did not feel were worthy of showing anyone. A helpful tactic might be gained from the iconic painter Georgia O'Keeffe, who once famously gathered up all the work she had done which she considered a failure (or at least not consistent with her most successful work) and burned it in a big bonfire in her back yard. If you don't want to burn a failed piece, at least take a moment to assess what you have learned and then put it away without beating yourself up.

Sculptor Jan Kirsh says that artists need to embrace the lessons learned from failure. Once while in the middle of a presentation for a class critique, Jan's sculpture of an ear of corn fell over and it was ruined. She had spent days painstakingly creating each kernel of corn. She went back and remade the piece again. The second one was better than the first. She, like many other artists, expressed the idea that every project taught them something for the next one. In fact, everything we do in life, whether it is a success or a failure, prepares us to do the next thing. Ultimately, we each have to directly face our successes and failures. Learn what you can from yours and discard the rest.

5. Listen and respond to the muse that is calling you.

Most of the artists I talked to have a persistent case of inspiration. Painter Geraldine McKeown talked about how artists just cannot help seeing the whole world as potential subject matter. The late writer Nora Ephron, famously quoted her mother who wrote movie screenplays based on her family and friends: "Everything is copy." With so many possibilities available, artists have to learn to tell the difference between flights of fancy and what ideas are worth pursuing. A good idea is like a puzzle in our brain which seems to demand a tangible solution. Once it is solved we dream up another one and get to work on it.

Lots of artists express anxiety about those times when they were creatively blocked, when no ideas seem to come. The only effective remedy seems to be to keep busy until the ideas return. In many businesses supervisors will say: "If you have time to lean, you have time to clean." When I get stuck, I straighten up my work space or go for a long drive or a hike. It is also a good time to practice technique or to try experimenting with materials. Before you know it your "muse" will be whispering new ideas in your ear.

6. Be yourself.

Impressionist painter Denise Dumont talked to me about how brushstrokes are like fingerprints. Every artist makes their own unique sort of marks on paper or canvas. Anyone can, with some instruction and some practice, force their hands to imitate the technique of a master. But, once you become a little comfortable with that, the next step towards real artistry is to simply appreciate the way your own hand makes a mark and allow your own soul to shine through the story you are telling. What makes something our own work of art, is to use creative techniques to say something about our own experiences. It may be as simple as: "I think this is beautiful." Remember, our lives teach us more than practicing any technique. Most art teachers will rightly tell you that you will not have matured as an artist until you have lived enough to have something to say with your art.

I have had a lot of people give me the same unsolicited advice after seeing a piece I did that they liked: "That's really great. You should just do paintings like this (boat, horse, bird etc.). You would make a lot of money doing them." It is wonderful when you get any kind of praise, but my response, sometimes out loud sometimes not, is that it would be a crushing defeat for me as an artist to do the same thing over and over again every day. Don't get me wrong. It is nice to get such a compliment. But I may as well give up my art and work as a file clerk, if I were to chain myself to just one idea. My advice to other artists would be: Don't let flattery alone, or criticism for that matter, dictate the direction of your work. Have confidence that your inner vision has value.

7. Find the right balance for you.

Self-help books are filled with advice about finding balance in our lives: balance between work and family, between personal needs and the needs of others. Lately I have been saying that perhaps if I had been more selfish and demanding I would have had more success as an artist. The truth is I have always been in a struggle to find a healthy balance of following that insistent creative muse and being the best wife, mother, daughter, sister, friend, and coworker that I can be. It is an ongoing personal battle. And, it has not always been a fair fight. Despite my efforts, I am sure there are those who would say I have lost out to being selfish on more than one occasion.

Artists who need to make a living, (and who doesn't?) must reconcile doing work that is both commercial and personally satisfying. I know of some artists who have set a ratio for themselves. For every two or three works that are strictly commercial, they allow themselves the reward of doing one strictly for themselves. For a fulltime artist who follows that strategy, the commercial work can become their "day job" and the other work becomes their "real art". Some are able to shift the ratio to favor personally rewarding work over the necessary and mercenary. The person who is able to make their daily work both a commercial success and an authentic reflection of their creative vision is truly lucky.

One artist I met told me that to choose just one medium was like asking her to eat on only potatoes and nothing else. She was a weaver, a painter, and a glass artist, among other things. Working in many mediums allows her to tell many stories in many ways. I could really relate to her comment because my own creative pursuits have at times been "all over the map" so to speak. I learned from all the artists I met that the goal is not to be continually balanced, but to take a longer wider view of things. Come back to the center from time to time and tend to what has been neglected. Things even out eventually.

8. Do it for yourself. Just do it.

Two of the most common pieces of advice my interview subjects gave for people new to making art were: "Do it for yourself not anyone else." And, "Just do it no matter what challenges you may have." There will always be a reason to do something more practical. What makes someone a "real" artist inside is that need to create which cannot be resisted or denied. When someone is willing to suspend propriety, and resist the expectations of others, they have taken the first courageous steps toward living their dreams out loud.

Several of the artists I met were embarrassed that they were still making art at their kitchen tables, that they did not have dedicated studio space. I told them that they were not alone, that I too often have had to work this way. I tried to encourage them with the story of a former student of mine. She did not have a place at home to make art and did not enjoy a lot of support from her family for her art. She had a fulltime clerical job and was responsible for most of the family housework. She kept her art supplies and artwork in the trunk of her car. She worked on her paintings primarily while attending classes and workshops in her "spare" time.

I am not sure there was anything I could have taught this woman about technique. Her work was amazing and beautiful. We, her friends, often expressed dismay at her situation. But she made it clear to us that she was at peace with it. Not painting was not an option she was willing to live with. So, she kept making art within the other constraints of her life. I have deep admiration for her dedication.

I suspect that I will never fully master all those lessons that I studied at the "Delmarva School of Art". I keep learning new aspects of them. During the last few months, as I began to devote more time to my painting again, I decided I would practice my technique on topics which are fun, even silly, specifically - mermaids. They helped me regain a sense of play with the medium. Now I am continuing to strive for new levels of excellence and I am moving on to other subjects that have meaning for me. I have more stories to tell. So, stay tuned. Thank you for reading this one.

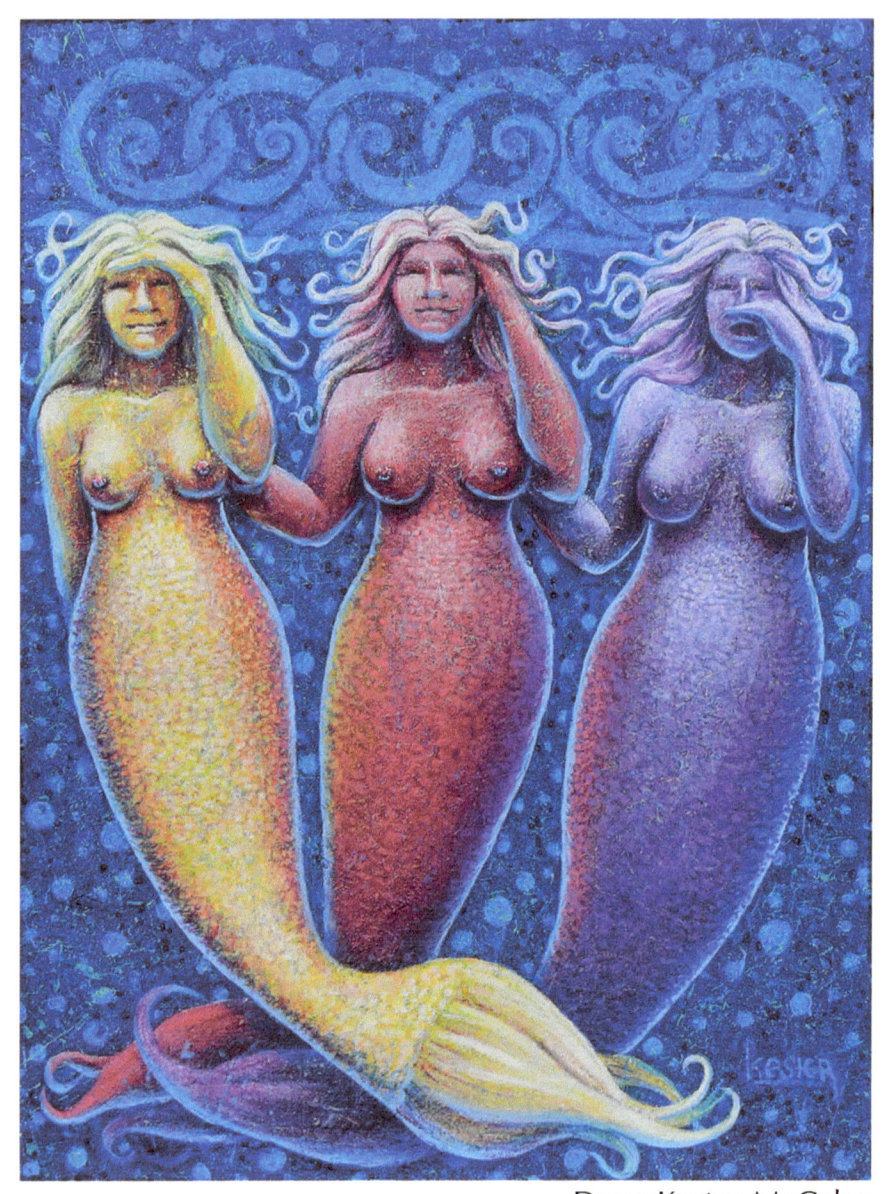

Dana Kester-McCabe
Sea Monkeys: See Love - Hear Love - Speak Love
(2017) Acrylics

About the Author

Dana Kester-McCabe is an artist and writer with over forty years of creative experience in website development, video production, print design, writing, and painting through her freelance business Moonshell Productions.

Dana recently served as host, executive producer, writer, and photographer for the Delmarva Almanac, a local online culture magazine and a radio show for two seasons on NPR stations WSCL and WSDL in Salisbury, Maryland. She has written materials for religious education, juvenile fiction, nonprofit public relations, commercial advertising, political opinion, and local journalism.

Dana has two grown children and lives with her husband on the Eastern Shore of Maryland.

Afterword

Art can be a wonderful part of our lives. I hope this book will inspire you to get involved in the arts where you live. Support your local artists. Buy their work. They have so much to offer: beauty, joy, and insight. Go to your town's monthly art stroll. They are great fun. Take an art class even if you think you have no talent at all. You will meet interesting people and learn something about yourself. Give the gift of art to your children at home and by supporting it in your schools. They will be better for it and so will you.

My hope in publishing this book is that it will encourage art lovers to further discover, support, and invest in the fine arts here on Delmarva. I also hope that it will inspire artists at all levels to continually raise the bars of excellence and authentic expression with their work. And, just maybe after reading this, someone who has secretly wanted to make art will find the courage to actually give it a try.

This book has a companion website where you can find the original video interviews with the artists in this book and links to them online. The site is a great resource for art lovers and artists whether they are visitors or locals. It has links to a variety of galleries and exhibit spaces, arts organizations, and the bigger annual competitions here on Delmarva. There is also a list of public parks, gardens, and other places which can serve as creative inspiration for budding and fully bloomed artists alike. Stop by and find out more:

delmarvaschoolofart.info